John Henry "Doc" Holliday

A Simple Matter of Survival

By R. Olin Jackson III
B.A., M.Ed.

Published by Whippoorwill Publications, LLC
Roswell, GA 30075

ISBNs: 978-0-578-35861-1 (hc); 979-8-987-2286-9-2 (pbk)

Library of Congress Control Number: 2023921413

Publisher's Cataloging-in-Publication Data
provided by Five Rainbows Cataloging Services
Names: Jackson III, Ralph Olin, 1951- author.
Title: John Henry "Doc" Holliday : a simple matter of survival / R. Olin Jackson III.
Description: Roswell, GA : Whippoorwill Publications, 2024. | Also available in ebook format.
Identifiers: LCCN 2023921413 (print) | ISBN 979-8-9872286-9-2 (paperback) | ISBN 978-0-578-35861-1 (hardcover)
Subjects: LCSH: Holliday, John Henry, 1851-1887—Biography. | Georgia—History. |
Outlaws—West (U.S.)—Biography. | Holliday family. | Earp family. | United States—History—
Civil War, 1861-1865. | BISAC: BIOGRAPHY & AUTOBIOGRAPHY / Historical. |
HISTORY / United States / State & Local / South (AL, AR, FL, GA, KY, LA, MS, NC,
SC,TN, VA, WV) | HISTORY / United States / Civil War Period (1850-1877)
Classification: LCC F594.H74 J33 2024 (print) | LCC F594.H74 (ebook) | DDC
364.1523/092—dc23.

Author of:

A North Georgia Journal of History, Volumes I – IV
Georgia Backroads Traveler
Tales of the Rails in Georgia
Moonshine, Murder, & Mayhem in Georgia
Mystery & History in Georgia, Volumes I & II
Some Genealogy Keys to Some Georgia Family Trees
Memories of Army Life and MPs of the 529th

Cover streetscape painting of John Henry Holliday by Tatiana Mack "Yaneya Art," Alpharetta, Georgia.

Copies of Whippoorwill Publications, LLC books are available online at Amazon.com; BarnesandNoble.com; IngramSpark.com; and other fine booksellers.

Contents

"We're all travelers in this world. From the sweet grass to the packing house; birth 'til death. We travel between the eternities."

- Robert Duvall

A Fayetteville, GA Home: Playground of Doc & Mattie

As of this writing (2023), John Henry "Doc" Holliday has been dead for almost 135 years, but his legend today is more profoundly and widely-known than ever before. He was born in Griffin, Georgia, and spent a fair amount of time in the Atlanta area, visiting with his uncle's family and later practicing dentistry.

Many Southerners have often claimed that historians – particularly historians from the North – were little more than myth-makers when it came to documenting "factual" information about the South. Invariably, outside historians – rather than sticking to writing about the history of their own region – choose instead to "document" Southern history, where, instead of sticking to the facts, they all-too-often write from a jaundiced perspective, "creating" and re-writing Southern history.

In fairness, even though Northern writers and documentarians all too frequently write inaccurately about Southern history, Southerners, while not revisionists of their own history, nevertheless invariably choose to embellish that history. When the two forces are combined, a myth of epic proportions is quite often the end product.

Victoria Wilcox, one-time chairwoman of the Holliday-Dorsey-Fife House Association of Fayetteville, Georgia, once asserted that the "Doc" Holliday of Western lore is in many ways just such a myth.

"I don't think John Henry (Doc) ever wanted to be a gunfighter," Wilcox asserted in an interview. "I believe what he really wanted was the kind of (refined) life his uncle lived right here in Fayetteville. He was even named after his uncle – Dr. Holliday – who was a medical doctor."

The "Atlanta" Hollidays

Doc's uncle was Dr. John Stiles Holliday, a Fayetteville physician. "John Stiles was the first of the Holliday family to obtain a college degree. John Henry was the second," Ms. Wilcox added, as she quickly ticked off facts about the famed gambler/gunman. Over the years, Wilcox stockpiled a wealth of information about the Hollidays, growing to be known as an authority on the subject.

"The Holliday House is the 'most intact' ante-bellum home in all of present-day metro-Atlanta," Wilcox noted proudly. "What I mean by intact is that when you walk in, you stand on the original Georgia heart-pine floors that have been there since the house was first built. Very little has been altered in the home since Dr. Holliday first lived here. Plumbing wasn't even added until the 1940s."

The Holliday home, as it exists today, has been around since 1855, but the original structure was probably built

Dr. John Stiles Holliday was the uncle of John Henry "Doc" Holliday of western fame. This artist's rendering of John Stiles was created circa 1860. (Collection of Morgan DeLancey Magee)

even earlier than that, perhaps as early as 1846 when John Stiles Holliday first purchased the property.

"In the vernacular, the original dwelling would have been considered an 'I-frame home,'" explained Wilcox. "A formal entry flanked by two rooms, one on each side with a stairway leading to two more rooms upstairs."

Prior to moving in with his family, Dr. John Stiles Holliday remodeled the house. Without aid of an architect, he added six massive Greek columns to the front verandah. He also added four more rooms to the rear of the home, making a total of four rooms downstairs and four upstairs. And nearby, he cultivated a vegetable garden and a small orchard to provide some of the family's foods.

Famous Connections

The old home has other interesting roots beyond that of the Holliday family. Prior to occupation of the home by his family, Dr. Holliday agreed to allow students at the new Fayetteville Academy to use the then-new home as a boarding house. The Hollidays therefore did not actually take up residence in the home until 1857.

Annie Fitzgerald, the grandmother of Margaret Mitchell, famed author of the international best-selling novel *Gone With The Wind*, attended Fayetteville Academy as a young girl. As a result of this family experience, Mitchell would later send her *Gone With The Wind* heroine, "Scarlett O'Hara," to the "Fayetteville Girl's Academy," modeled after Fayetteville Academy in Mitchell's imagination.

The esteemed author's writings in association with her family experiences did not stop with Scarlett either. Her cousin from the Fitzgerald clan – Martha Anne "Mattie" Holliday – was the prototype for Mitchell's character of "Melanie" in the famed novel.

Mattie spent her childhood in Fayetteville and nearby Jonesboro. The Hollidays were a close-knit Irish clan, and family gatherings at the Holliday home were common.

It was during these and other such gatherings that a strong bond between young Mattie and John Henry (Doc) Holliday was established – a relationship about which there has been much speculation and romantic intrigue over the ensuing century.

Cousin Mattie

Only twenty months older than Doc, Mattie Holliday was his playmate and companion during assemblies at the Holliday house in Fayetteville. The secrets the two shared as children formed the basis of an intimacy that lasted throughout their lives. The depth and breadth of this relationship and its exact details are not known today, and perhaps have been lost to posterity, but the subject nevertheless has been fodder for much myth-making over the years.

In the 1993 major motion picture *Tombstone*, starring Kurt Russell and Val Kilmer, a mythical Doc confesses to Wyatt Earp that an affair with a cousin caused her to enter a convent and him to leave his home in disgrace. This, quite possibly, is a somewhat accurate portrayal of the actual circumstances.

Cousin Mattie, born December 14, 1849, was the daughter of Robert Kennedy Holliday. She was raised a Catholic, and became a nun at the age of 34. She took the name "Melanie" in honor of Saint Melaine, who, after marrying a kinsman, sought a life of complete devotion to God. Did Mattie take the name Melanie because she was in love with her own cousin, Doc?

"Family members in the past have been reluctant to admit that any such relationship actually existed between John Henry and Mattie," confessed Wilcox, "but the myth that he left Georgia simply because of poor health is questionable. John Henry supposedly left Georgia for a higher and dryer climate to combat the tuberculosis with which he had been diagnosed, but he traveled to Dallas, Texas, which is actually a lower elevation, geographically, than even Atlanta, and is almost as humid.

"In all likelihood, the Doc-Mattie relationship probably did in fact play a role in his decision to leave Georgia," Wilcox added. "After all, many people with advanced cases of tuberculosis such as was suffered by Doc were going to Florida for treatment in those days."

In fairness, many travel decisions made by Holliday the last ten or fifteen years of his life were not logical ones, and seem to have been little more than

Mattie ("Sister Melanie") Holliday, was John Henry Holliday's first cousin, and has been the object of much speculation in his life down through history. Some historians have maintained that a love affair between the two ultimately sent him out West and her to a convent. (Susan McKey Thomas collection)

aimless wandering in search of adventure and yet another gambling opportunity. To attach any special significance to his travels from 1873 and later would be pure folly.

Summer Love

It is entirely plausible that Doc fell in love with his favored cousin the year he turned sixteen. In 1864, in an effort to escape the Union army which was advancing into north Georgia, Doc's father had moved the family from Griffin (in north Georgia) to Valdosta (in extreme south Georgia).

After the war, around 1867, Doc spent one summer with Mattie's family in Jonesboro, and it quite possibly was during this period that their romance blossomed. Even long after she became "Sister Melanie," Doc maintained a strong bond with his cousin, often

The impressive home built by Dr. John Stiles Holliday in Fayetteville, Georgia, still stands as of this writing (2023). It has been in existence at least since 1855, and quite possibly was built as early as 1846 when Dr. Holliday first purchased the property. Dr. John Stiles Holliday was the uncle of John Henry "Doc" Holliday of western fame and diagnosed the tuberculosis in his nephew circa 1873. It was at this home that young John Henry spent much time in his youth forming a bond with his cousin Mattie which ultimately had a profound impact upon both their lives.

writing to her of secrets only the two of them shared.

Who knows today if these letters and missives were love letters? In point of fact, it will probably never be known now to a certainty. Mattie considered the letters ultra-private, and later burned them to avoid any revelation of the details within them in the future.

According to family legend, Mattie later regretted the destruction of the letters. *"Had I not destroyed most of his letters, the world would have known a much different man than the one of Western lore,"* she later confessed.

According to records, Doc went on to study dentistry at the Pennsylvania College of Dental Surgery, graduating in 1872. He was planning happily for his future, totally unaware he would be gone in a scant fifteen years.

After graduation, Doc practiced dentistry briefly in Atlanta. It was at about this time that he was diagnosed with tuberculosis, a dreaded disease for which there was no cure at that time.

A Move To Dallas

It was shortly after learning of his disease that Doc departed for Texas, quite likely sometime in 1873. One can only imagine the pain and despair his fate must have caused him. He probably had suffered a tragic love affair from which there was no recourse, and then shortly thereafter had been informed that he had contracted a fatal disease.

After arriving in Dallas, Doc must have needed funds, for he set up a dental practice there. At this time, the West was still a wild frontier in many respects. In short order, Doc had become a part of this wildness, exacerbating the traits of drinking, gambling, and carrying of firearms. He, however, also continued to practice dentistry.

According to O.K. Corral chronicler Paula Marks, Doc soon garnered a reputation as *"one of the touchiest drunks in the West."* Wyatt Earp himself declared *"Doc's fatalistic courage . . . gave (him) the edge over any out-and-out killer I ever knew."*

Doc was arrested January 1st, 1875, for shooting at a saloon-keeper in Dallas. According to the January 2, 1875 issue of the **Dallas Herald**, *"Dr. Holliday and Mr. Austin, a saloon keeper, relieved the monotony of the noise of fire crackers by taking a couple of shots at each other yesterday afternoon. The cheerful note of the peaceful six-shooter is heard once more among us. Both shooters were arrested."*

Doc apparently decided at that point that it was time to leave Dallas, and drifted on to Fort Griffin, Texas. There, he was indicted by a grand jury for *"gaming in a saloon,"* along with Hurricane Bill, Liz, Etta, Kate, et alle, and charged with keeping a *"disorderly house."*

"Kate," "Bat," and Wyatt

This "Kate" named in the indictment was the first published link between Doc and the female who eventually became known in Western lore as "Big Nose Kate." Along with Doc, Mary Katherine "Kate" Harony would become widely known for her "adventures."

From 1875 to 1878, little is accurately known about Doc's wanderings. It is known, however, that he eventually traveled with Kate to Denver, Colorado, where he began dealing a popular card game called faro.

By late 1877, Doc and Kate were back in Fort Griffin. It was here that he first met another drifter who would gain fame in the West by the name of Wyatt Earp. Doc's illness and frail health no doubt caused him to prefer New Mexico, Texas, Kansas and Arizona in the winter months, saving the gambling opportunities in the gold and silver mining towns in Colorado and parts northward for the summer months.

By 1878, Doc had arrived in Dodge City, already preceded by a rather substantial reputation as a dangerous man. It was here that he played poker in the Long Branch Saloon, and rode in posses with Wyatt Earp and Bat Masterson. Masterson, who disliked Doc and later became a writer of sorts, penned a number of articles – after Doc's death – which portrayed the Georgian in a negative light.

According to an article Masterson wrote in a 1907 issue of **Human Life** magazine, Doc *"went from Dodge to Trinidad, Colorado, where, within a week from the time he landed, he shot and seriously wounded a young sport by the name of Kid Colton over a very trivial matter. He was again forced to hunt the tall timber and managed to make his escape to Las Vegas, New Mexico, which was then something of a boom town. . ."*

Masterson later wrote that *"Holliday had few friends anywhere in the West. He was selfish and had a perverse nature – traits not calculated to make a man popular in the early days on the frontier."*

Whatever the circumstances, the John Henry Holliday described by William Barclay "Bat" Masterson did not match the description of the Southern gentleman of record back in Georgia. And in retrospect, it is famously-easy to ridicule and criticize an individual when that individual isn't around to defend his good name.

Interestingly, though highly critical of Holliday's "perverse nature" as Masterson described him, it was Masterson himself who, after becoming so unpopular and troublesome, was run out of the city of Denver, Colorado, and told never to return.

Uncovering The Secrets of the Holliday Home in Griffin, GA

Recent investigations and research on John Henry Holliday have revealed some captivating details, particularly as concerns his former homes in Griffin, Georgia.

Bill Dunn was a man on a mission. A distant cousin to Griffin native John Henry "Doc" Holliday, Dunn made it his goal in life to publicize the truth about his famous forebear – the Southern gentleman as opposed to a reckless outlaw – for posterity's-sake.

As simple as that might seem, it, in fact, is considerably difficult to achieve, especially when dealing with a Western legend whose fascinating life has inspired innumerable interpretations, movies, books and other media, as well as exaggerations and defamation in these media.

Dunn, however, must have had luck on his side. Since he began researching Holliday in the 1980s, he managed to uncover quite a bit of previously unknown information pertaining to the dentist-gambler and his Griffin roots.

For instance, Dunn discovered evidence that Holliday actually practiced dentistry in Griffin – a detail heretofore unsubstantiated. He also has researched two "Holliday graves" in the local

Dunn, however, must have had luck on his side.

cemetery believed to be those of Doc's father's slaves, and two other graves in the same cemetery which he maintains are "more than likely" those of Doc and his equally-elusive father.

During their research, Dunn and his fellow Doc "enthusiasts" also discovered the actual site upon which the dentist/gunman's boyhood plantation home in Griffin once stood. "This find," said Dunn, "is the most satisfying of all. While the other discoveries happened along the way, this is the one I've been pursuing for decades."

Hitting The Jackpot

John Henry was born August 14, 1851, in Griffin, a west-central Georgia town with a population of barely 22,000 even at the dawning of the 21st century. He was the only living child of Henry Burroughs and Alice Jane McKey Holliday. Prior to his birth, a sister, Martha Eleanora, had died at the age of six months.

John Henry was born in a house which once stood at the corner of what today is

The infant John Henry Holliday from a tinted daguerreotype, 1852 (from the collection of Karen Holliday Tanner).

The petite grave of Martha Eleanora Holliday, John Henry Holliday's infant sister who died at the age of six months, is located at Oak Hill Cemetery in Griffin. She died in 1850, the year before her famous brother was born. (Photo by Jackie Kennedy)

Tinsley and North 9th Streets, according to Dunn. A modest brick residence now occupies this corner lot. The current residents of this home quite possibly have no clue today that they live on ground once occupied by a Western legend.

John Henry's father had served in both the Indian and Mexican wars by the time his only son was born. Ten years later, the elder Holliday joined the Confederate Army and fought in his third war.

During the decade in-between these two wars, Henry Burroughs had worked as a druggist in Griffin and served as the first elected clerk of court there. His family – though not wealthy – was stable and socially prominent. They attended Griffin's First Presbyterian Church where records today indicate the infant John Henry Holliday was baptized at the age of seven months in 1852.

When John Henry was two years old, the family moved to a 148-acre plantation in rural Griffin. It is the location of this homestead that had eluded

historians in the 20th century, and that Dunn had long hoped to find.

"I'd been looking for twenty years," he said. "I'd get close but just couldn't pinpoint the location." Destiny, however, literally walked through his door one day, and Dunn said he still gets goose bumps talking about it.

An employee of Spring Industries – which, as of this writing, owns the former Holliday plantation property – had been researching water locations at the site when he reportedly came across a copy of a 140-year-old map. "Bill, I think you'll be interested in this," the worker said as he conversed with him that day.

To his amazement, Dunn discovered the map described in detail the lay of the land of *"Camp Stephens,"* a Griffin-based Confederate Army camp

The lot upon which this more modern home stands today at the corner of Tinsley and North 9th streets in Griffin was owned by Doc Holliday's father, Major Henry B. Holliday, and is believed to have been the site of the Holliday home in which Doc lived until he was two years of age. (Photo by Jackie Kennedy)

Henry Burroughs Holliday, John Henry's father, was photographed circa 1852, while the family yet lived in Griffin, Georgia, south of Atlanta. He would ultimately refugee southward to Valdosta, Georgia, to escape the oncoming Union Army juggernaut of Gen. William Tecumseh Sherman who was headed for Georgia in his infamous "March to the Sea."

which existed in 1862. Major Henry Burroughs Holliday had sold 137 of his original 148 acres to the Confederate Army for construction of the camp, leaving 11 acres for his family's residence. There, on the map, was clearly listed *"H.B. Holliday's second home."* Confederate Private Asbury H. Jackson had given the original map to Doc's mother in March of 1862.

"You search for something for years, then somebody just walks in and hands it to you," Dunn smiled, still incredulous. To top things off, the fellow who presented him the prized map was a man who had somewhat irritated him the year before at *"Doc Holliday Days,"* an annual event in Griffin.

"This newspaperman asked me about Doc and I pointed him to several experts who were attending the event," Dunn explained. "Instead of interviewing them, he goes up to this fellow (the eventual map-bearer) who had a tattoo of Doc above his ankle. He asked the guy, 'How do you feel about having someone who drank too much, gambled and killed people depicted on your body?'

"Instead of defending Doc, this fellow responded, 'It don't bother me. I do a little of that myself, except for the killing.' Needless to say, I was a little perturbed with him," Dunn confided.

Keeping his frustration to himself, though, Dunn said his resolve paid dividends in the end when the tattooed fellow presented him with the map in the summer of 2002.

Walking Hallowed Ground

The map had barely exchanged hands when Dunn solicited help from two friends – fellow members of the Doc

Holliday Society (of which he serves as president) – who were in town that August weekend for Holliday's annual birthday bash.

With Gene Carlisle, a Holliday researcher who has penned a manuscript on the Western legend, Dunn set out hiking. Using the map as their guide, the men followed the old Macon and Western Railroad line toward the house site, battling tree branches, vines and undergrowth as they searched for the site of the old home-place.

Veering off the historic railroad tracks, the men cut their way through one particularly dense area of undergrowth for a short distance before stumbling upon a scattered pile of ancient fieldstones which the men now believe were used in the foundation of the Holliday house.

"Gene," Dunn uttered, barely able to breathe. "I think we've found it."

The next day, Keith Reed – Holliday Society member and the third explorer – entered the wooded area himself at a different angle, hoping to prove Dunn's assumption correct.

"He said he was practically eaten alive by redbugs," Dunn smiled, "but he stepped off the map's directives and landed on the exact same spot, confirming it as the former Holliday home-place."

The site is about two miles from Griffin's town square. Interestingly, Dunn says some earthworks from Camp Stephens – just as they appeared during the Civil War – remain in the vicinity adjacent to the home-site.

As the war worsened for the South in 1864 – and with the Confederate camp barely a hop, skip and jump from the Holliday home – it does not take a rocket scientist to understand why Major Holliday moved his family to Bemiss (a south Georgia town near Valdosta)

Major Henry Holliday, Doc's father, was the first clerk of court in Georgia's Spalding County. The historic courthouse, which still stands in downtown Griffin as of this writing (2023), included an office for Holliday in the 1850s. (Photo by Jackie Kennedy)

that same year, almost simultaneously as William T. Sherman's Army was marching toward middle Georgia.

"Surely," said Dunn, "the major (medically discharged in 1862 due to 'watery dysentery') reckoned Sherman would march right by his home with destruction in mind. Seeking safety, he undoubtedly moved his family farther southward, eventually settling in Valdosta where he acquired more than 2,000 acres and ultimately served four terms as the city's mayor."

John Henry's Georgia

Back in Griffin, Georgia, tangible reminders of Doc's days in this town are abundant even today if one knows where to look. Bill Dunn happily points these out to curious visitors to his town today.

There is John Henry's birthplace on Tinsley Street and the Holliday plantation. There's the former site of First hatred and violence sparked all relationships between Whites and Blacks of the pre-Civil War era, Dunn – just as other Southern historians – asserts that nothing could be further from the truth. He said this was particularly true in regard to the Holliday family.

"Doc, in fact, probably even picked up his card-playing skills from a slave girl – Sophie Walton," Dunn continued, "with whom he often played as a child. She resided at his Uncle John Holliday's farm. According to family tradition, it was Sophie who taught a young John Henry the skills he later used to support himself as a gambler after tuberculosis robbed him of the ability to practice dentistry. She reportedly taught him a number of the tricks of the trade, such as 'skinning' cards and 'the put-and-take' technique of dealing cards."

Doc, the Dentist

One of the most intriguing "Doc sites" in Griffin is the building where he may have practiced dentistry after leaving the practice at which he was working in Atlanta. In a 1940 *Griffin Daily News* article, Judge L.P. Goodrich noted that his father had known the Hollidays. The article goes on to state, *"Doc Holliday returned to Griffin after the war and practiced dentistry here in an office in the old Merritt building."*

It is a matter of public record that John Henry, in fact, once was part owner of the Merritt building, known in the 1870s as the "Iron Front building." He had inherited half of the property from his mother's estate, and her family – the McKeys – had claimed the other half.

"They actually drew a line down the middle of the building, separating the two halves," Dunn added. "Doc later sold his half for $1,800.00, which was a good price for that property back then."

Bill Dunn, a distant cousin to Doc Holliday, rests his foot upon a fieldstone believed to have been a portion of the foundation of the famous gunman's boyhood home in Griffin. Major Henry B. Holliday purchased and moved his family to this site in 1853, and John Henry lived at this site from age 2 to age 12. (Photo by Jackie Kennedy)

Presbyterian Church where he was baptized. (The Griffin Fire Station stands on this site today.) There's the old Iron Front Building which he once owned and in which he is believed to have practiced dentistry. There also is the old courthouse in Griffin where Major Holliday served as clerk of court. And at Oak Hill Cemetery, there's the final resting place of Doc's sister – and possibly other graves of even more importance.

A bit beyond John Henry's sister's grave are the graves of Mariah and Harry Holliday, a black couple who, according to Dunn, probably were slaves on the Holliday plantation.

"By all indications," said Dunn, "the Hollidays were good and decent people who cared for their workers." Despite a common tendency to believe that

(Equivalent to approximately $43,000.00 in 2023 dollars.)

Dunn said he feels certain Doc practiced dentistry in an upstairs office at the Iron Front. After graduating from Valdosta Institute in 1870, Doc had entered the Pennsylvania College of Dental Surgery from which he was graduated in 1872.

He subsequently returned south and worked for Dr. Arthur C. Ford in his dental practice in Atlanta on Alabama Street, while living with his Uncle John Stiles Holliday a short distance away. *(Interestingly, a portion of this office building has survived on the old portion of Alabama Street preserved in the former "Underground Atlanta" attraction.)*

While Ford attended the Southern Dental Association Conference in Richmond, Virginia in the summer of 1872, Dr. John Henry Holliday was left in charge of Ford's practice. "When the elder dentist returned, Holliday was left with time on his hands – time to commute to Griffin to operate his own dental practice," said Dunn.

"If he practiced here, this is where he did it," Dunn said, pointing to four holes in the original wooden floor situated in strategic spots to accommodate a dental chair of that time period. Equally interesting is a tin cylinder discovered under a loose floor

Dunn said he feels certain Doc practiced dentistry in an upstairs office at the Iron Front.

"If he practiced here, this is where he did it," Dunn said.

plank in this same upstairs room at *Holliday's Portions & Elixirs*, a restaurant that once occupied the old Iron Front building.

"He probably used this for dental supplies or possibly even a hideaway for money," said Dunn who researched the cylinder, stamped *"Great Northern Manufacturing Company, Chicago,"* and found it to be of Civil War-era vintage. Great Northern carried dental supplies among many other items.

"It sure does lend credence to the possibility that Doc practiced dentistry here for two or three months before heading out West," Dunn concluded.

Resting In Peace, But Where?

While history claims that Doc Holliday is buried in Glenwood Springs, Colorado, persistent rumors through the years have suggested that Major Henry B. Holliday in fact brought his son's body back to Georgia for burial. It's one rumor in which Dunn places some credence.

"Yes, I sincerely believe that," he stated emphatically. "Knowing Southern history as I do – and knowing the major had the motive, the money, the mode of transportation, and nothing to stop him – I believe he brought Doc back and buried him under this oak tree," Dunn said, pointing to a stately

FORT STEPHENS – Though the full details of this site have been lost through the passage of time, this rare historic print reveals a portion of the troops at this Confederate training encampment near Griffin, Georgia, in the early 1860s. This facility was located one-half mile east of the railroad and two miles north of Griffin. It was the presence of this camp adjacent to his plantation and the looming threat of a Union Army invasion of Georgia, which caused Major Henry B. Holliday to move his family – including a young John Henry – to south Georgia. (Confederate Stamps, Old Letters, and History)

oak in Griffin's Oak Hill Cemetery. "Until someone proves otherwise to me, I'll believe Doc's buried right here beside the major."

The unmarked twin graves at Oak Hill are compelling. Set off to themselves, they are covered by unassuming concrete slabs with no engravings. Dunn theorizes that Major Holliday either went to Colorado himself or sent a relative to retrieve his son's remains, then buried his boy under the now-massive oak.

Interestingly, a heavy-duty ancient nail is driven, rock-solid, into a sprawling root of the oak, centered above what Dunn believes to be Doc's grave. Dunn conjectures the major quite possibly could have hammered in the nail and used it to work a pulley to lower his son's casket into its final resting place.

"The nail-pulley mechanism would have enabled him to accomplish the two-man job on his own," said Dunn. It's a plausible theory if you believe the major wanted his boy's gravesite to be kept a secret.

Supporting his belief that father and son are buried in Griffin are these notes of interest: 1) While Doc is said to be buried at Glenwood Springs, Colorado, the marker in the cemetery there reads, *This memorial dedicated to Doc Holliday who is buried "someplace" in this cemetery.* It is a fact that no one today knows the actual gravesite – if it exists at all – in Glenwood Springs containing Holliday's last remains. 2) While some Valdostans believe Major Henry Burroughs Holliday is buried in that Georgia town, no one knows the exact location of his gravesite either. Dunn finds it difficult to believe that the grave of a man of his prominence (veteran of three wars and a four-term mayor) would be unknown and unmarked today if indeed it did exist in Valdosta. 3) The twin graves in Griffin are in the Thomas family plot. Dunn said the Thomas and Holliday families were socially connected and the Thomases may very well have acceded to Major Holliday's request and agreed to the anonymous burial of Doc Holliday in their plot.

"Why can't the folks in Glenwood Springs point to Doc's grave?" questioned Dunn. "It's because it's not there. Major Holliday had the motive and the means to bring his boy back to Griffin. A man of Southern heritage would want his son buried near him, and removing him to an anonymous location would prevent the vandalism that surely would have followed had Doc's gravesite been revealed."

Gentleman From Georgia

They say you can take the boy out of Georgia but can't take Georgia out of the boy. John Henry Holliday left the South and lived out West as "Doc" Holliday the final 15 years of his life, but did he long for home?

An 1882 *Atlanta Constitution* interview with Holliday family friend Lee Smith indicates he did. When asked if Doc ever spoke of returning to Georgia, Smith responded, *"He would be back here today but for fear of being handed over to the Arizona authorities."*

By the 1880s, however, the West had claimed Doc Holliday as its own. He ultimately died in a Colorado hotel on Nov. 8, 1887, tuberculosis finally defeating him.

It's a matter of public record that John Henry died out West, but, if Bill Dunn's theory about the two graves at

Sophie Walton was a female slave born in January of 1856 on a farm owned by the Walton family. Sophie enjoyed a higher status than the other slave children because she had been fathered by Mr. Walton. Several years after the end of the U.S. Civil War, Mr. Walton was no longer able to care for all of his slaves, and arranged for Sophie to go live at the home of Dr. John Stiles Holliday, John Henry's uncle, in Atlanta. Among her many skills, Sophie was extremely adept at cards, and taught John the skills he later used as a professional gambler out West. Sophie was photographed here in 1895 in Atlanta.

Oak Hill Cemetery in Griffin, Georgia is correct, the noted gunman did, indeed, come home to Georgia a final time.

Bill Dunn said he likes Tombstone (Arizona) Historian Ben Traywick's description of Doc Holliday best: "He was an orchid in a cactus patch."

Dunn said he once received a call from Traywick when the Tombstone historian was working on his book, *John Henry: The Doc Holliday Story*.

"He asked me to help and I asked him how he intended to portray Doc," Dunn recalled. Traywick replied, "As the true Southern educated gentleman that he was."

"What can I do to help?" Dunn said he responded. Published in 1996, the book, to Dunn's delight, "does nothing to discredit Doc."

Known best for teaming with the Earp brothers to defeat the Clantons and McLaurys in the 1881 gunfight behind the O.K. Corral, Doc Holliday became a larger-than-life legend. Over the next century, stories of him would range from fact to fabrication with his reputation as a ruthless gunman dominating. Numerous publications and Hollywood movies would paint the picture of a merciless killer with murder in his heart.

"The facts," said Dunn, "dictate a different personality – that of an educated gentleman who never abandoned his Southern roots." Either way, the intrigue of Doc Holliday continues, even as it did a century ago.

"This guy from Buckhead called to get information for a report his 11-year-old daughter was doing on Doc," said Dunn. "He said she was infatuated with him and that after seeing the movie *Tombstone*, she could recite all of actor Val Kilmer's dialogue in the movie."

While some insist on portraying John Henry as a killer without a conscience, Dunn vows the dentist from Griffin fired a weapon only when he had to, and he never

Either way, the intrigue of Doc Holliday continues, even as it did a century ago.

became comfortable with killing. The handsome ash-blond, blue-eyed Georgian who departed his home for the drier climate out West to slow the stranglehold of tuberculosis was most likely "a very typical young guy, mischievous with an out-going personality," says Dunn.

The Stuff Of Legends

Dunn appreciates the comparisons which sometimes are drawn between himself and his famous relative, but he's also serious about the preservation of John Henry Holliday's legitimate legacy.

"Being a relative has little to do with it," Dunn added. "I've got this thing about Hollywood and history. History is more exciting than Hollywood could ever make it. Why they have to exaggerate and fabricate things just doesn't make sense to me."

While his findings do shed light on the history of Doc Holliday, the mystery which pervades his persona is certain to dog this Western legend as long as Hollywood's cameras roll. Whether he's viewed as a Southern gentleman, a Western gunman, a man with a death wish, or a man who dared death to do him in, Doc Holliday remains the stuff of legend. Regardless of later depictions and Hollywood tripe, he began his life as an educated and cultured son of the South from Griffin, Georgia, who lived an honorable and captivating life and died an honorable death.

Doc Holliday remains the stuff of legend.

A Valdosta, GA Refuge from the Dogs of General Sherman

His legacy as a gambler and fearsome gunfighter in the old West is secure. Lesser known, however, are the details of John Henry Holliday's life during his adolescence in Valdosta, Georgia.

I f there is one sure thing that can be said of the legacy of John Henry "Doc" Holliday, it is that there is virtually no agreement whatsoever about many aspects of his life. No one was more aware of this than author Susan McKey Thomas of Valdosta, Georgia, the legendary gunfighter's first cousin once removed, who spent the better part of three decades trying to sort through competing popular mythologies for the truth.

"I have no ax to grind, and I have no one to protect," said Thomas in an interview in 1999. Her sharp wit and elegantly groomed appearance offered only a small hint of her age. "I'm just trying to get to the truth," she stated matter-of-factly.

Thomas's historical odyssey began in 1972, when members of the Lowndes County Historical Society were asked to submit summaries of their family backgrounds for inclusion in the society's records. Wading into waters fraught with hearsay and legend, Thomas and Albert Pendleton, secretary of the Society's newsletter, discovered what Thomas called "many shocking inaccuracies" about her famous forebear.

Research Discoveries

"One of the first things we found out was that Wyatt Earp was little more than a pimp," explained Pendleton. Indeed, historians support the claim that several of the Earp brothers and their wives – some of whom were prostitutes themselves – ran brothels across the Old West, but then that was not unusual at all at that time. In fact, it was more the norm than the exception.

Doc Holliday himself "took up company" with a prostitute – Katheryn Haroney (a.k.a. Harony) – also known as "Big Nose" Kate Elder. Holliday's adventures in the West, however accurate the retelling of them may or may not be, are reasonably well-known. Less-known, however, is the story of the Holliday family in Valdosta, where John Henry spent much of his adolescence.

Even here, Thomas and Pendleton ran into myriad conflicting stories, enough so that it took 18 months of painstaking research before Thomas felt she could reliably submit her family story to the historical society for future readers and researchers.

The work of Thomas and Pendleton, in fact, turned up so much information that their contributions took the

Major Henry Burroughs Holliday moved to Valdosta, Georgia, circa 1864, to escape the anticipated devastation of north Georgia by invading Union troops. Pictured here is the Holliday home in Valdosta, where a young John Henry spent his adolescence attending Valdosta Institute and hunting and fishing in the surrounding countryside.

form of a book, *In Search of the Hollidays*, published in 1973 by Little River Press. "We found out so many things that it just seemed like we needed to write them down," Pendleton said.

The book turned out to be something of a local sensation, and in the years that followed, copies were sold to history buffs from almost every state and several foreign countries. From that effort, the desire to know more about her famous cousin drove Thomas to an on-going investigation of much of the Holliday mystique, including the eight years in which John Henry lived in Valdosta.

Early Valdosta Days

The story of John Henry Holliday in Valdosta, Georgia, begins early in 1864, when his father, Major Henry Burroughs Holliday, brought his family to a settlement of about 1,500 people in what then was a virtual wilderness in extreme south Georgia. It was far from the Holliday family home in Griffin, Georgia, but it was a safe haven from the looming Federal siege of Atlanta and the advancing Union Army of Gen. William T. Sherman.

Major Holliday, a veteran of the Creek Indian wars, the Mexican War and the U.S. Civil War, had retired from military service and found refuge in a large tract of land northeast of Valdosta, near a tiny fiefdom known as Bemiss. By that time, the Hollidays had already reared to manhood a young orphan – Francisco Hidalgo – brought home by a compassionate Major Holliday in 1849 after the Mexican War.

In earlier years when he had lived in Griffin, Georgia, Major Holliday – as he

Valdosta Institute, a private school, provided young John Henry with an impressive education in the classics. The date of this photo is unknown, but it quite likely was taken circa 1870s, possibly even during the time-period in which this school was attended by John Henry.

was formally known – had worked as a druggist. In the largely unsettled south Georgia countryside, however, he became an entrepreneur, opening a plant nursery, planting vineyards and promoting the production of pecans, an undertaking which today has grown into a major agricultural industry stretching from Valdosta westward across the clay hills of southwest Georgia and on to the north of the state. Indeed, Georgia now produces more pecans than peaches. It, in fact, produces more pecans today than any other state in the Union.

Ms. Thomas said the young John Holliday, 12 years old when he arrived in Valdosta, was remembered by area residents as being nice looking and slightly built, with piercing blue eyes and blonde hair.

Later biographies recorded John Henry's gracious manners as well as his unpredictable temperament, but Valdostans remembered only a well-mannered adolescent who dressed neatly and grew into a young man known for his ability on a dance floor amidst the musical talents of his McKey relatives.

The McKey Family

History correctly records that young John Henry was well-educated. He was schooled at the private Valdosta Institute which, as reported by Louis Pendleton in his *Echo of Drums*, stressed classics and taught *"advanced branches."* Headmaster Samuel McWhir Varnedoe (How's that for a name?) set up a challenging curriculum including Greek, Latin, French, advanced English, mathematics and history.

Following the end of the Civil War, the Holliday/McKey family clung to a semblance of affluence when most other

17

Southern families and former business-men were relegated to poverty. The young Holliday's three McKey uncles – James, William and Thomas – bought a large tract of land in the lakes area along the Georgia-Florida border south of Valdosta in an area known as Bellview.

The McKey property, known as "Banner Plantation," is said to have been a favorite haunt of John Henry, who reportedly spent much of his adolescent years hunting and fishing on the property. His favorite uncle, Tom, who was only 10 years older than John, often accompanied him.

Years later and a world away out West, John Henry assumed the alias Thomas "Mackey" (as the family surname was then spelled) for a short time, presumably because he had encountered legal problems or conflicts of another nature, and needed to disguise his identity.

"I don't know why he did that," Susan Thomas said in her 1999 interview. "He wasn't famous, really, until the O.K. Corral." Many historians would reply, however, that despite the fact that he hadn't yet been involved in the famous gunfight in Tombstone, John Henry was, nevertheless, becoming known as a testy gunfighter even by the time he reached Dodge City, and had already reportedly been involved in more than one altercation.

Whatever the case, back in south Georgia, what seems to have been an idyllic childhood for John Henry was shattered by tragedy in the form of the unexpected serious illness of his mother. Alice Jane McKey Holliday gradually lost her strength and endured a lingering and torturous state of health until September 16, 1866, when she finally passed away from the same illness – tuberculosis – which would later haunt and prematurely-destroy John Henry.

The youngster, who had dearly loved his mother, reportedly was devastated.

As if his mother's death was not bad enough, family stories maintain that John Henry was shaken even worse by the almost immediate remarriage of his father to another woman a mere three months after his mother's death. Major Holliday married Rachel Martin, 23, a young lady who was less than half his age and only nine years older than John Henry.

Reconstruction Trauma

Other outside factors also impacted the Holliday family in Valdosta. Following the U.S. Civil War, the turbulent years of Reconstruction took a serious toll on the Holliday family's financial fortunes. An abusive Federal occupation with its associated retributive and punitive legalities for anything "Southern" set the Holliday circumstances back even further.

Rachel Martin's family owned farmland which adjoined the Holliday property. Records indicate that the Martins purchased the Holliday tract, and that Major Holliday's father-in-law gave to his daughter a house in Valdosta at 405 Savannah Avenue. The Holliday family – including young John Henry – soon relocated to this new address.

Never one to take defeat easily, Major Holliday immediately began working to recover the family fortune. He opened several businesses, including a furniture store. The *1870 Census* lists him broadly as "general agent." Eventually, Thomas says, Holliday regained all of his former properties, but he never fully recovered financially.

Major Holliday also gained some acclaim in the political arena in his community. He served four terms as Valdosta's mayor.

While his father was beginning to prosper once again, the younger Holliday began pursuing the behavior for which he would become more widely known later in life. Local tradition maintains – incorrectly – that he eventually fled town after running afoul of Federal officials.

Young John Henry was in fact accused of being associated with – and indeed may even have been the mastermind of – a plot to destroy with explosives the then-Federally-operated Lowndes County Courthouse. In the Reconstruction South, the county courthouses often were taken over by occupying Federal forces in order to set up a legal sanctioning body for the doling out of punishments of White Southerners. Though a subsequent newspaper account of the incident (in which John Henry supposedly was involved) lists the names of five participants who were accused of the crime, John Henry, was not one of those identified or even implicated in the crime.

Major Holliday was one of five men appointed by the Valdosta City Council to draw up a plan to deal with the unrest in the area during Reconstruction according to Ms. Thomas. One could surmise that John Henry's family connections could have protected him from prosecution in the courthouse incident, but any such conclusion, like so many others involving Doc Holliday, would be pure conjecture at this late date.

Swimming Hole Incident

Ms. Thomas said young Holliday was also involved in a shooting incident reportedly prompted by his discovery of a group of Blacks in a riverside swimming spot he and his friends often frequented near the confluence of the Withlacoochee and Little rivers at the

John Henry Holliday was photographed here shortly after his graduation from the Pennsylvania College of Dental Surgery in Philadelphia. Totally unaware of the fatal illness within his body at this time, he assumed a long – and no doubt prosperous – life lay before him. He lived a scant 15 years after this photo was taken, most of which was spent in Texas, New Mexico, Arizona Territory and Colorado, suffering desperately from the ills of tuberculosis. He would die in Glenwood Springs, Colorado in 1887. (Photo by O.B. DeMorat)

old settlement of Troupville. In reality, however, what modern America wished to conveniently convert into yet another "racial issue" perpetrated by a "racist" Southerner, actually amounted to little more than young Holliday defending himself after being attacked by the Blacks when he had demanded that they leave the property.

Once again, this "racial incident" occurred during the Reconstruction years, when tensions were extremely high. At that time, many Blacks reveled in their new-found superior social status, often intentionally inflaming a situation by flaunting their ability to violate long-standing Southern social mores. Rather than calm the circumstances, Reconstruction-elected officials often fanned the flames of divisiveness with abusive penalties for trumped-up (and often completely false) charges against Southern Whites.

Ms. Thomas said the story involving John Henry was confirmed by Thomas McKey, John's uncle. In the late 1920s, Thomas says McKey related the incident involving John Henry to writer Stuart Lake who was working on what later would become a controversial book about Wyatt Earp.

"He told the story of (McKey and Holliday) going to a swimming hole which Whites had traditionally used as a spot for swimming and leisure activity, and that was when they discovered a group of Blacks in the water," Ms. Thomas related. "[John Henry] first ordered the trespassers out of the water, and after being abusively spurned and threatened, he then turned to retrieve his pistol." One of the Blacks, however, had quickly armed himself when he saw that Doc was turning for his gun.

According to local tradition, a Black federal officer was killed in the incident, but in the interview with writer Stuart Lake, Thomas McKey firmly denied anyone was wounded or injured in any way. Here again, the supposedly "murdered Black Federal officer" almost certainly was little more than a fabrication designed to conveniently paint Holliday as a racist in order to fan the

> *One of the Blacks, however, had quickly armed himself when he saw that Doc was turning for his gun.*

flames of divisiveness in a conquered South.

Today, there is no microfilm available for the **Valdosta Times** newspaper during the period in question, but McKey's assertion of John Henry's innocence is given some credence by the fact that there is no evidence of any such incident in the records of the Lowndes County Superior Court for the years 1866 through 1873, and the occupying Federal authorities, as well as Reconstruction-elected officials (as explained above), were always quick to take advantage of any opportunity to punish any White Southerner involved in any incident with even a hint of racial edge. All of the above supposition of the swimming hole incident, however, might not have even occurred at all in Valdosta, as will be explained.

On To Dental School

Despite the trouble John Henry may or may not have initiated as a teen, he went on to graduate from the Valdosta Institute in 1870. Later that year, he applied and was admitted to the Pennsylvania College of Dental Surgery from which he was graduated during the 16th annual graduation ceremonies of March 1, 1872.

During his studies in Pennsylvania, John Henry occasionally returned to work his required "preceptership" with Valdosta dentist Lucian Frederick Frink. Ms. Thomas said there is some evidence that Holliday performed dental work in Valdosta in October of 1871, and it is believed he returned home for a brief visit after his graduation, but a short time later, he struck out for Atlanta to open a dental practice in that newly-rebuilt city which was just then recovering from the destructiveness of the Union Army forces in Georgia.

Though he did not know it at the time, even as he left Valdosta, the newly anointed "Dr." Holliday was no doubt already a doomed man. Within a year, he would be diagnosed with tuberculosis, a disease for which there was no treatment until the mid-20th century. It was the same disease which had killed his mother.

This diagnosis was a fate that possibly sent John Henry to the drier climate of the West for health reasons, and, within the space of four more years, found him – depending upon who one wishes to believe – becoming a playfully subversive gambler, or a studied gunman, who had a "very short fuse" when larger and much stronger individuals sought to bully him or physically take advantage of his slight stature. Ms. Thomas, in the sincere opinion of one who has sought the truth for so very long, places her famous cousin somewhere in the middle of these two extremes.

Historians and researchers today maintain that John Henry almost certainly had been infected with the tuberculosis bacterium years prior to the diagnosis of his disease. He might possibly have contracted it from a dental patient upon which he trained early in his college education. However, in reality, he more than likely contracted it from his mother, although Thomas says there obviously is no way to prove that today. Each day, his advancing illness robbed him of still more of his strength.

Interestingly, Francisco Hidalgo, the Mexican youth raised by the Hollidays is also known to have died of the dreaded disease, providing still more strong evidence that the seeds of Doc Holliday's eventual demise in a Colorado

An infant John Henry Holliday was photographed with his mother, Alice Jane McKey Holliday circa 1852. Even as a small tyke, John Henry demonstrates an unsettling gaze. Both he and his mother – from whom he quite possibly contracted the fatal disease – would die from the tuberculin bacteria. A cure for the dreaded malady would not be discovered until almost 100 years later in 1943. (Craig Fouts Photo Collection)

hotel in 1887 were sown long before that time, either in Griffin or Valdosta.

Leaving Home Forever

Once he left Valdosta, Doc Holliday apparently considered his break with south Georgia to be permanent. There is no evidence that he ever returned to visit, even though there is evidence that he strongly yearned for a reconnection with his family.

A legend within the Holliday family maintains that Major Holliday arranged a meeting with his son while in New Orleans at a Confederate veterans' convention in 1885, and begged the ailing John Henry to come home to his family. Whether the meeting ever took place or not is, predictably, unverifiable today.

What can be said with certainty, however, is that if the estranged father and son had such a meeting, it was their last. Doc Holliday did not return to Georgia, and by 1885, he was so sick that he could barely manage to support himself in the gambling profession any longer – and to him, it was literally a profession, not a game. After he ceased practicing dentistry, gambling was his full-time occupation, and when healthy, he was quite adept at it.

Though often merry – and sometimes even comical in nature – John Henry's otherwise testy nature caused him to be involved in more than one serious altercation shortly after his migration to the West. In a locale which thrived upon reputations, the legend of Doc Holliday as a gunman quickly became established, and any return to his home in Georgia where his family's reputation might be tarnished by his disreputable identity became impossible for the wandering former dentist to even consider.

During her research of John Henry Holliday, Susan Thomas did make one very interesting – and very unexpected – discovery. The orphan – Francisco Hidalgo – left behind a legacy of his own in neighboring Berrien County in the form of the "Edalgo" family, of which he was the progenitor.

After more than a century, that piece of information came as a complete and total surprise to the Edalgos who continue to live in this south Georgia county even as of this writing, and who previously had been unable to trace their ancestry beyond their local community.

Remnants In Valdosta

Today, the Holliday legacy is alive and well in Valdosta, even if the Major and Doc are long gone and the Holliday name itself has all but disappeared in the community.

Major Holliday, in addition to serving as mayor of the city, rose to additional prominence in that town. He served as secretary of the Lowndes County Agricultural Society, secretary of the Confederate Veterans of Camp Troup, census enumerator, and superintendent of local elections. He even had a street named for him near the original site of the Holliday house off Savannah Avenue.

The Holliday house in Valdosta – John Henry's adolescent home – lives on as well as of this writing (2023). In the 1970s, the aged structure was purchased by Valdosta businessman Dick Davis and moved to a new location off U.S. Highway 41 South. A few years later, the home was given a new lease on life when it was purchased by a local couple and moved to one of the new subdivisions which sprawl far to the northwest of town.

After its relocation, the house was extensively renovated, although many of its original aspects were preserved and incorporated into the new additions to the structure. It was later purchased and occupied by Dr. David Johnson and his wife, Susan, at 2605 Pebblewood Drive in Valdosta. Its disposition beyond that status is unknown today.

After he ceased practicing dentistry, gambling was his full-time occupation

Myths About His Georgia Life

Though much of his life has been documented for posterity, a number of gaps still exist in the collective record of his life and times.

One would just naturally anticipate that a person as "celebrated" as is John Henry Holliday would have little unknown information in the story of his life – even with a man as secretive about his personal life as was he. Holliday, however, seems to be the exception to the rule, as is the case concerning a number of aspects of his life. Many have speculated and offered supposition regarding these "unrecorded" and therefore unknown details, and therein lies much of the intrigue of this famed Old West figure from Georgia.

The Swimming Hole Incident

Much has been made over the years of a presumed "incident" between John Henry Holliday and several Blacks at whom he supposedly directed gunfire in an argument over a favored "swimming hole" at some point in his youth. Just as with many circumstances which make a grand story if one is able to "reinvent" them into an event involving a racial component, this one also has been blown out of proportion if not completely misrepresented. It just naturally makes the story and character that much more controversial if "the race card" can be played.

First of all, much of the knowledge of this presumed "incident" was initially presented as fact by John Henry's cousin, Mrs. Clyde McKey White, and subsequently repeated by William Barclay "Bat" Masterson, Walter Noble Burns

and others. While not denying that such an "incident" may, in fact, have actually occurred, the individuals making this contention either used faulty information, or were simply unreliable as sources – or both.

Mrs. McKey's *"Papa told me. . ."* account regarding Doc and the incident appears highly unlikely when examined in the light of day. "Papa" quite likely told his daughter many things, but that doesn't necessarily make them true, and Mrs. McKey simply was not present herself to witness whatever incident actually occurred, so she could only repeat what she "thought" her father had stated scores of years earlier. This isn't exactly the concept upon which "factual information" is based.

And by the time "Bat" Masterson got around to repeating what was little more than a rumor from Mrs. McKey, he (Bat) was little more than a derelict alcoholic who had earlier disgraced himself in towns in the West such as Denver, Colorado, to the point of being permanently ejected and barred from those municipalities. Having retired to the New York City offices of the *Morning Telegraph* newspaper, Masterson had been forced to support himself with inflated "remembrances" of his days in the West and the famed gunmen with whom he had interacted.

In May of 1907, Masterson produced an article for publication in

Human Life which introduced many readers to the presumed swimming hole incident involving Holliday. Master Bat had little evidence other than the rumor-mill to support his contention about Holliday and a matter as serious as murder. *"The indiscriminate killing of some Negroes in the little Georgia village in which he lived was what first caused him* (Holliday) *to leave his home,"* Masterson wrote. *"The trouble came about in rather an unexpected manner one Sunday afternoon – unexpected so far, at least as the Negroes were concerned."*

The article Masterson penned for *Human Life* can only be described today as a critically unfair fabrication regarding Holliday which unjustly became a portion of the Georgian's permanent record. Masterson's dislike for Holliday is well-known, resulting mainly from a distaste for the Georgian's quick temper and periodic alcoholic rages. Bat Masterson had no proof whatsoever to back up his contention.

In retrospect, this incident could have involved Blacks. It could also have, to the contrary, involved only Whites. Holliday's actions – if they occurred at all – could easily also have been justifiable, but it makes a much more dynamic story if it can be conveyed in a dramatic racial context.

First of all, this supposed racial incident which was published in Masterson's fourth installment of his *"Famous Gunfighters of the Western Frontier"* series supposedly occurred after the Holliday family had relocated to "Valdosta," Georgia, to escape the onslaught of Gen. William T. Sherman's troops through Georgia in the final year of the U.S. Civil War. Masterson, avoiding specifics for understandable reasons, stated it occurred *"near the little town in which Holliday was raised. . ."*

Repeating the rumor in 1927, Walter Noble Burns in his *Tombstone: An Iliad of the Southwest* was the first to specifically establish Valdosta and the Withlacoochee River in that vicinity as the site of the incident. The "respected writer," William Barclay Masterson, had stated that it occurred in *"the little town in which Holliday was raised,"* so Burns immediately reasoned that Masterson had to be referring to Valdosta/Lowndes County and the Withlacoochee. But is this accurate?

Since there were no other swimming holes – as it were – which John Henry might have conveniently frequented in the vicinity of his home in Lowndes County except along the section of the Withlacoochee River flowing through his McKey uncles' property (which adjoined the Holliday property), and with the logistical requirements of physical travel being what they were in the 1870s, logic would dictate that a popular swimming spot frequented by the McKey and Holliday boys would not have existed anywhere except upon the McKey property. The Holliday property had no swimming holes.

And from whence did the Blacks at which John Henry supposedly fired his weapon originate? Neither the McKeys nor the Hollidays owned slaves at this time in Georgia, since it was the post-Civil War era, and no Blacks lived upon the McKey or Holliday properties. The combined acreage created a reasonably extensive tract of land with few if any neighbors in what then was basically still an unsettled wilderness in south Georgia. So from whence did the manufactured Blacks come? No one has the answer. More speculation.

The time-line for the occurrence of this incident is faulty as well. A pre-February, 1872 swimming hole shooting

24

incident in Valdosta must be ruled out, since Holiday's uncles – William H. and Thomas S. McKey – *did not even purchase their Withlacoochee River acreage until February of '72*. And a date *after* that February is even more unlikely. The shooting (if such occurred) almost certainly had to have occurred *prior to* John Henry's entry into the Pennsylvania School of Dental Surgery in Philadelphia, wherein he was preoccupied with his education and, immediately afterwards, the cultivation of his professional career.

John Henry was involved with his education at the Philadelphia school from 1870 to 1872 – much too far from home to be involved in swimming hole trivialities. From March thru October of 1871, the Georgian fulfilled the requirements for his eight-month dental preceptorship (apprenticeship) with Dr. Julian Frink. On November 6, 1871, Doc's classes resumed in Philadelphia and continued until graduation in March of 1872.

Following the conclusion of his educational pursuits, John Henry immediately began the pursuit of his young professional life. On April 3, 1872, the *Georgia State Dental Society* opened its fifth annual convention in Atlanta, which Doc almost certainly attended to establish important contacts for his budding career. Though no written account of his actual presence at this event has been discovered, he, as a young and ambitious medical professional, would have been loathe to have missed this opportunity to rub shoulders with Georgia dental professionals.

Lest we forget, the sole aim of John Henry Holliday at this time in his young life was the pursuit of the profession in which he had invested so much time, energy and money. By this point, he had

no thoughts whatsoever of idle playtime in a swimming hole in the wilds of south Georgia, much less of foolhardy gunplay with trespassing Negroes.

And what of the public records – the newspapers and court documents – which would have recorded a shooting of this nature? No such incident is mentioned anywhere in the Lowndes County news media nor court records. Why is that? Could it be due to the fact that the incident didn't occur at all in Lowndes?

It also is quite possible that in 1872 or even in 1873, John Henry Holliday returned to his original boyhood home of "Griffin," Georgia, to practice dentistry there for a short period of time after inheriting the "Iron Front Building," a substantial commercial structure in the town. *(Readers please see Page 32: "John Henry's Last Georgia Possession" in this publication.)* His mother had left the property to her son in her Will, and John Henry quite possibly briefly maintained a dental practice therein.

On April 3, 1873, the *Georgia State Dental Society's* annual convention was held once again – this time in Columbus, Georgia. Dr. Arthur C. Ford was elected Society President, and he had already become significant in Holliday's life, providing him with his first opportunity for a professional dental practice through a partnership. The **Columbus Daily Sun** published a list of all dentists practicing in the state prior to August 24, 1872. Listed among the 143 dentists was *"Haliday, John H., Atlanta,"* where he practiced in concert with Dr. Ford.

At some point around 1873 or shortly thereafter, John Henry Holliday became acquainted with the gambling trade and the debauchery so prevalent in the vicinity of his early employment with Dr. Ford. In short order, drinking, gambling, and womanizing took over his life and his professional dental practice "took a back seat." He soon became so dissolute that Dr. Ford apparently was compelled to sever his professional relationship with John Henry, sending Holliday's life spiraling out of control and ultimately converting him into a vagabond bereft of hearth and home.

The combination of all the above circumstances left virtually no opportunity for the aforementioned "swimming hole incident" – as described by Mrs. Clyde McKey White and mimicked by William Barclay Masterson and Walter Noble Burns – in this portion of his life either, nor, in all likelihood, for it to have occurred in Valdosta at all. In point of fact, the most likely point at which something of this nature "might" have occurred would have been much earlier in Doc's life at the Holliday family home in Griffin (*not on the Withlacoochee in Valdosta*), where a younger John Henry spent the first twelve years of his life.

Born in Griffin in 1851, John Henry lived for the first two years of his life in a small home on that town's Tinsley Street. In October of 1853, Henry B. Holliday – Doc's father – purchased a plantation one and one-half miles north of Griffin where the youngster spent the following ten years of his life. As stated, this property would have been a much more likely locale for a "swimming hole incident." Even more telling, this property included a large natural spring (and associated popular swimming spot) at which a shooting incident quite easily could have occurred.

In March of 1862, Private Asbury H. Jackson (CSA infantry) sent a letter home to his mother from Griffin's Confederate Camp Stephens. Included in this letter was a finely-drawn map which intricately detailed Camp Stephens,

a substantial military training facility for the Confederacy. Mrs. Jackson and her heirs somehow had retained possession of the map down through time until it eventually was discovered in a dusty file drawer by an individual named Mike Watson in 2002.

Without Pvt. Jackson's map, the specific location of Henry B. Holliday's home – which had disappeared over the ensuing years – on his plantation might never have been known. Spalding County Deed Books A and B, provide a detailed description of the acreage included in the plantation, but no information regarding the Holliday home itself.

Despite Pvt. Jackson's detailed map, the aforementioned plantation site – still wholly undeveloped right up to the 21st Century – had become completely obscured with the passage of years by dense undergrowth and forested expanses, causing any actual relocation of the former Holliday home to be extremely difficult. Even the ancient steel rails (which still exist to this day) from the historic *Macon & Western Railroad* had been completely hidden by all the heavy overgrowth of bushes, vines, scrub pines, and decayed vegetation. Nevertheless, after extensive research by *Doc Holliday Society* President Bill Dunn of Griffin and an associate, the foundation stones of the former Holliday home as well as the steel rails of the railroad were eventually uncovered and revealed.

Henry B. Holliday had initially purchased 147 acres in 1853 near Griffin situated north of the city proper and along the east side of what today is the long-abandoned *Macon & Western Railroad* tracks. Holliday subsequently sold 136 acres at this site to Confederate authorities for the creation of Confederate Camp Stephens and retained 11 acres for his home. He then purchased an additional 278 acres outside the bounds of Camp Stephens for a total of 289 acres in his plantation where he planted Sea Island cotton and corn. Henry Holliday's 289-acre plantation was then bounded on the west by the *Macon & Western Railroad*, and on the east by Camp Stephens.

"Holliday Creek" which rises from the large natural spring on Henry's property, almost certainly was the site of the much-debated "incident" – again, if it ever occurred at all – although it would, by virtue of the time-period – have involved a much younger John Henry Holliday who could not have been more than 12 years of age at the time.

According to Bat Masterson's 1907 *Human Life* article on the swimming hole incident, *"The Negro boys were informed that in the future, they would have to go further down the 'stream' to do their swimming, which they promptly refused to do, telling the Whites that if they didn't like existing conditions, that they would have to hunt up a new swimming hole."* Defiance of this nature from Black slaves in 1860s Confederate Georgia – particularly as involved someone else's private property – would have been highly unlikely, which, again, makes the occurrence of this presumed incident suspect at best – but it, nevertheless, made a good story.

If this incident in fact did occur, there were a number of different scenarios which might have transpired. At the top of the list would have to be the possible altercation between John Henry Holliday and the aforementioned Blacks. The "swimming hole," however, was located on Holliday property, so if this did occur, young John Henry would have been well within his rights to order any trespassers from his father's

property. And if said trespassers threatened the youngster, he would have been well within his rights to fire warning shots to ward them off, particularly in Confederate Georgia.

Scenario number two would involve a group of Whites trespassing at the swimming hole who likewise refused to depart the Holliday property and who likewise were warded off with warning shots. There was at least one White family – that of William and Lucinda Bates – who lived on property directly across the railroad tracks from the Holliday tract who had male children of ages 17 and 19, as well as two other males of ages 12 and 14 in the household, all of whom would have been of the "bully" age at this time, and no doubt often patronizing the swimming hole. John Henry, once again, would have been well within his rights to demand their departure from the spot if this formed the basis of the scenario. It, however, would not include the racial component, so it no doubt would have gone with little mention beyond the actual occurrence of the incident.

And finally, if this incident ever occurred at all (because as detailed above, the original reference sources used by those describing this presumed incident were, at best, highly suspect or nonexistent), it most certainly did not involve any deaths or injuries, since no mention is made of any such injuries or deaths in either the newspapers or court records of either Lowndes or Spalding counties or the towns of Valdosta or Griffin, and John Henry – if involved at all – almost certainly would have been more than justified in his actions.

Also as explained above, all of this would have been occurring with a John Henry Holliday who was not more than 12 years of age, since the Holliday family only resided in Griffin for the initial twelve years of John Henry's life, so he would have been barely more than a youngster at the time anyway, even though he quite likely would have been well-versed in the use of firearms by age 12.

These things being said, the "swimming hole incident" and its highly-publicized racial component quite likely did not occur at all. It would therefore appear that this presumed event was, in all probability, nothing more than a sensationalized incident fabricated around a non-existent racial component.

The Atlanta Dental Practice

Much of Atlanta's former Whitehall Street is today named Peachtree Street (since it, in fairness, is basically the south end of that famed avenue). The building at the southeast corner of Alabama and Whitehall/Peachtree streets is not the one which once housed the dental offices of doctors Ford and Holliday, but it is the site at which John Henry "Doc" Holliday set up his first "recorded" dental practice in Georgia.

In Doc's day, Peachtree Street ended and Whitehall Street began at the east-west juncture of the *Macon & Western Railroad* at this site *(which interestingly is the same railroad which passed through his father's property at John Henry's boyhood home in Griffin, Georgia).* "Railroad Gulch" still exists at this site in Atlanta today, but it is covered over and virtually obscured on the east side by viaducts and bridges which hide much of the rail yard which was so visibly portrayed in the epic and major motion picture *Gone With the Wind*.

Unbeknownst to many, remnants of the former site of Holliday's practice were still extant in the 1960s and '70s entertainment complex once known as *Underground Atlanta*. Cobblestoned portions of Alabama and Whitehall streets still exist there beneath the viaducts even today, as do the lower level/basement sections once comprising some of Atlanta's original commercial buildings.

In Doc's day (1870s), the Whitehall Street district formed the "Deadline" section of town "on the south side of the tracks." Saloons and bordellos proliferated there, and, in a short period of time, these came to be heavily patronized by John Henry. The legend of the "Doc Holliday" known in Western lore was born and bred in this neighborhood. Did his eventual debauched behavior in Atlanta begin after his discovery of the fatal disease he carried in his lungs? Possibly. Likely.

The *Hanleiter City Directory* for the year 1870 lists a total of twenty saloons and bars in Atlanta. Fourteen of the twenty are clustered in the blocks just south of the railroad on Alabama, Hunter (present-day Martin Luther King Street), Mitchell, Broad, and Whitehall Streets. The fourteen saloons are: *ME. Kenny, T.F. Grady, Dan Fleck, G. Hentschel, N.M. Robinson, Steadman and Kreis, J.L. Griffin, H. Muhlenbrink, M.E. Maher, D. Wallace, Michael Haverty, Frantz Eddleman, John Gaven,* and *Jake Emmel.* "Muhlenbrink's Saloon" was one of the storefronts which survived beneath the viaducts and which was later renovated and reused in the *Underground Atlanta* complex. This structure, quite possibly frequented by John Henry, likely still exists there even today.

In the years 1870 to 1874 (excluding 1873 for which there was no listing), a grand total of forty-six saloons operated south of Railroad Gulch. The bulk of Atlanta's non-Whitehall Street saloons

FORD DENTISTRY – The structure which housed Muhlenbrink's Saloon on Alabama Street (photographed here circa 1970) still existed and was used for many years in the entertainment venue known as "*Underground Atlanta*." This site was a popular attraction of 1960s and '70s Atlanta before the inner city's crime caused it to be closed. Approximately 150 years ago, in the summer of 1872, John Henry "Doc" Holliday, at the age of 21, had just graduated from dental school in Philadelphia, and was working in the Atlanta dental office of Dr. Arthur C. Ford on Alabama Street quite near to the site pictured here, adjacent to the old Atlanta rail yard. Holliday possibly even patronized Muhlenbrink's.

listed in *Hanleiter's* were located in the mid-town district just north of the railroad.

The exact time that the dissolution from drink, gambling, and womanizing took possession of John Henry's life is unknown today (yet another gap in his history), but it quite probably is fair to say it began with the severance of his professional partnership with Dr. Arthur C. Ford. At some point no more than a year after the initiation of their promising dental practice, Dr. Ford decided that he had erred in the assumption of a business relationship with his young protégé,

sending John Henry Holliday adrift into the unknown.

After alcoholism took over his life, John Henry apparently pursued the lure of the gambling tables to an even greater extent, until his depravities had robbed him of any financial security he might have previously enjoyed. At this point, his inheritance of the Iron Front Building in Griffin from his late mother became a much-needed sudden windfall which allowed him to continue without a steady job.

As explained above, he apparently made a brief attempt at resuming a professional dental career in Griffin, but it was short-lived. The incident or incidents which had culminated in the termination of his relationship with Dr. Ford apparently had poisoned any further hope for employment in Atlanta or environs. After all, no one wished to go into partnership with a drunken ne'er-do-well, nor did patients wish to have their teeth pulled or cavities drilled out by such a dentist.

Realizing that he needed to depart for a site where he might "begin anew," he set out for Texas

As a result, at some point, John Henry Holliday was forced to face the conclusion that Atlanta and Georgia held little to no further allure for him. Realizing that he needed to depart for a site where he might "begin anew," he set out for Texas, eventually winding up in Dallas.

Did this departure from Georgia coincide with his debauched behavior and the ruination of his professional career opportunities in Georgia; or was it the result of a tortured romance with his cousin Martha Anne "Mattie" Holliday; or was it in fact the diagnosis of his contraction of the terrible incurable disease known as tuberculosis which spurred his travel westward? We'll never know, because he kept few if any letters or records on matters of this nature, and the reason or reasons for his relocation to the West became yet another gap in the collective record of the life of John Henry Holliday.

Cousin Mattie Holliday

Much has been made down through history of the reason or reasons for the departure of famed Western gunman John Henry "Doc" Holliday from Georgia. It has been suggested that a primary motivation was a star-crossed romance with a cousin which sent her into a Convent for the remainder of her life and him into banishment from his home state of Georgia for the remainder of his life. The circumstances of his life have been the subject of speculation since the 1950s.

Mattie Anne Holliday, the daughter of John Henry's uncle – Robert K. Holliday – was Doc's soulmate and playmate in the early years of his life, and his confidant until the day he died on a cold winter day in Glenwood Springs, Colorado in 1887. She was the one to whom he told his secrets, and the one with whom he formed a bond which endured for the remainder of both of their lives.

How deep was this relationship? The blessed few inklings offered by John Henry during his lifetime revealed nothing more than an unbreakable bond strongly akin to – if not the actual condition of – deep and affectionate love.

John Henry talked of her sparingly to others during his lifetime, but from the scant comments he did make, it was clear that she was extremely important to his life and that he deeply regretted the fact that they had been separated for life.

Unbeknownst by many, John Henry and Mattie (or "Sister Melanie" as she became known after making a life-time commitment to a Convent) communicated often by letter. And Mattie saved all of these letters, right up until the time of John Henry's death, at which time, the letters were burned. She later regretted the action, stating, *"Had I not burned the letters, the world would have known a much different man from that described in books and magazines."*

So what happened? What caused Mattie to commit her life to a Catholic Convent and him to commit his life to that of an alcoholic gambler drifting across the Old West? We'll likely never know the answer to those questions either. Still more gaps in the collective history of John Henry "Doc" Holliday.

Actual Site of His Grave

Also contrary to popular myth and modern movie portrayals, Doc Holliday did not die in the Glenwood Springs "Sanitarium." There was no sanitarium in Glenwood Springs in 1887. Doc Holliday died in his room in the Hotel Glenwood.

Mystery seems to have followed Doc right into the grave. The actual site of his burial is not known today either. There is a Doc Holliday gravesite in Linwood Cemetery outside Glenwood Springs, but it is an acknowledged fact that many historians believe Doc Holliday is not buried there. Even the cemetery records state only that it is believed that he is *"buried somewhere in this cemetery."*

On the day of Doc's funeral, the weather reportedly was bitterly cold. Along with John Henry, one other recently-deceased gentleman was to have been buried in Linwood Cemetery on the same day. On the day of the burials, the trail up to the cemetery was completely impassable, and, as a result, Doc and the other deceased individual reportedly were buried by the side of the road *"somewhere along the route up to the cemetery,"* the intention being that they would be exhumed in the spring and re-buried within the actual cemetery.

The following spring, however,

things changed a bit. The individual buried beside Doc apparently had family in the Glenwood Springs area who readily paid to have their loved one dug up and re-buried in Linwood. Doc, however, had no family in the area, and according to reports, no one was forthcoming to pay the fee to have him exhumed and re-buried. He, therefore, according to most reports, was simply left buried beside the road.

As time passed, local residents came and went and the actual site of the grave of famed John Henry Holliday supposedly and surprisingly was forgotten. It was only in the mid- to late-20th century that local residents – realizing the historic and tourism-related value of Doc's burial site – began trying to re-locate his grave.

Despite considerable efforts toward this attempted relocation, the positive identification of John Henry's gravesite has completely eluded researchers and historians. Today, the mortal remains of Dr. John Henry Holliday from Griffin and Valdosta, Georgia, possibly exist beneath someone's back porch or in someone's yard on the route up to Linwood Cemetery.

Other accounts, however, differ with the above scenario. According to one, Doc's remains were indeed later dug up and re-buried in Linwood Cemetery, where they exist today. Another account maintains that they were dug up, but were transported – via the new railroad in Glenwood Springs – back to Georgia in the late 1880s, where they were re-buried in an unmarked grave in Griffin, Doc's birthplace. If the remains in the unmarked grave in Griffin are ever excavated and examined via DNA analysis and for a tubercular condition, a connection to John Henry might be finally established. Time will tell.

John Henry Holliday's Last Georgia Possession

It has stood in this middle Georgia town since the days of the Wild West. Indeed, it once was co-owned by one of the most famed old West icons of all time.

Dallas, Deadwood, Dodge City, Tombstone . . . . The names evoke images of the wild, wild West and the now legendary world of John Henry Holliday. "Doc," however, had another world as well – a Southern world in Georgia where he once lived and worked, and of which remnants still exist today.

These sites include landmarks like the home of his uncle, Dr. John Stiles Holliday, in Fayetteville, Georgia, where the future gunman often visited with his cousin, Mattie; the sites of the former Holliday homes in Griffin, Georgia, where he was born and lived the early portion of his life; the former Holliday home in Valdosta, Georgia, to which his family moved in the 1860s, fleeing the on-coming juggernaut of Gen. William T. Sherman; and the Griffin, Georgia office building – known collectively as "the Iron Front Building" and "the Merritt Building" – where a young Dr. John H. Holliday reportedly once practiced dentistry a short time.

It is a matter of legal record that the Iron Front building on Griffin's historic Solomon Street was a portion of John Henry's inheritance from his mother, Alice Jane McKey Holliday. When Alice Jane died in 1867, the building was passed to thirteen-year-old John, with his father, Henry Burroughs Holliday, acting as his guardian over the property until he became "of age."

A Family Rift

A short three months later, Henry Burroughs shocked the Holliday family by quickly remarrying. The unusually-quick remarriage understandably caused a rift within the family, which, in turn, also surprisingly caused John Henry's relatives on his mother's side – the McKeys – to file suit against the Hollidays in an attempt to reclaim what they felt was "McKey property."

The suit was brought by John Henry's (Doc's) uncle, Tom McKey, and was tried in the Lowndes County courthouse in Valdosta. Ironically, this is the same uncle who Doc so admired, and whose name he later used as an alias to disguise his own identity while in Colorado.

A short three months later, Henry Burroughs shocked the Holliday family by quickly remarrying.

Known in John Henry Holliday's day as "the Iron Front Building," this structure which still stands in downtown Griffin as of this writing (2023) was once partially owned by Doc Holliday. He inherited this building from his mother's estate upon her death, and briefly set up a dental practice here in the summer of 1872. It was at this approximate time that he quite likely learned of the tuberculosis he had contracted in his lungs. The prospect of a career in Georgia no doubt was soon dimmed for him at this point. In short order, he subsequently traveled to the western United States where he began life anew. (Photo by Jackie Kennedy)

Even more surprising is the fact that the case, *McKey vs Holliday*, ultimately proved to be at least a partially-successful suit, causing Alice Jane's estate to be divided equally between the McKey and Holliday families.

This unique settlement included the Merritt/Iron Front building in Griffin, of which ownership was likewise divided equally between the McKeys and John Henry. The legal solution had been to literally create a partition down through the middle of the building from roof to basement, with the eastern half being returned to McKey ownership, and the western half remaining as John Henry's legal inheritance. Though this suit and subsequent settlement obviously denied John Henry a substantial portion of his entitled estate, history does not record his reaction to the decision or to his McKey relatives who prevailed in the case.

It is likewise unknown today just how John Henry's mother, Alice Jane, came to own a substantial downtown Griffin property such as the

> *This unique settlement included the Merritt/Iron Front building in Griffin*

Tiffany Hinton of Griffin lifts a section of loose plank from the floor of an office in the Iron Front Building in which Doc Holliday is believed to have briefly practiced dentistry in Griffin. When she first discovered the hiding spot, Tiffany found a tin cylinder stored inside it. Research on this item determined that it was a Civil War-era container for dental supplies. The hiding spot almost certainly was used by "a dentist" in yesteryear, possibly even by Holliday himself. In front of this open space in the foreground, a drilled hole is visible. It is one of four such holes into which a dental chair of the style used in the 1870s quite likely had been fitted. (Photo by Jackie Kennedy)

Merritt/Iron Front building. It presumably had been in the family for a number of years, with inheritance by Alice Jane following the death of another member of her family who had owned it.

Impressive Asset

The Merritt/Iron Front was certainly a property worth fighting for. It was an impressive structure, two stories high with an iron infrastructure (and thus its name) beneath its fancy red brick façade. Both floors of the building had long multi-paned windows facing the street in Doc's day. They allowed the morning sunlight to stream into the rooms with their hardwood floors and pressed-tin trimmed ceilings.

At the rear of the main floor, a huge mechanical lift carried merchandise from the loading dock to the second floor offices. In Doc's day, the Iron Front was leased out as shop space to various businesses, and records have indicated it generated good income in rents.

Henry Burroughs Holliday continued his guardianship of the property until his son reached the age of 21 in the summer of 1872, at which time Doc was able to legally take possession of his inheritance. At that time, John Henry had just graduated from dental school in Philadelphia, and was working in the Atlanta dental office of Dr. Arthur C. Ford on Alabama Street in the vicinity of what once was the popular entertainment complex of the 1970s thru the 1990s known as *"Underground Atlanta."*

With his own office building, John Henry enjoyed the unique distinction of being able to immediately open his own dental practice in his hometown, Griffin. Nevertheless, his professional tenure in Georgia was, as explained above, short-lived.

John Henry registered his ownership of the Iron Front building in the Spalding County Deed Book in November of 1872. According to old-time Griffin residents, he also did a modest amount of remodeling to the building, adding an exterior iron staircase which rose from the alley beside the building up to the little second floor office where he set up his practice.

Validation of Doc's Griffin Practice?

According to researcher Gene Carlisle in his ***Why Doc Holliday Left***

Georgia, "It is possible that Doc Holliday – in 1872 or '73, returned to Griffin, Georgia, the city of his youth, and there practiced dentistry for a brief duration in an office in the Merritt Building (a.k.a. 'Iron Front Building') on Solomon Street. A vivid account, penned by the late Griffinite, Judge L.P. Goodrich, has withstood the test of time and numerous assaults by diligent researchers who failed to strike it down. Judge Goodrich's account is excerpted as follows:

"'One evening when I was a boy, my father looked up from the newspaper which he had been reading, and said, "Doc Holliday is dead." His tone indicated that he knew Doc Holliday, and that his death was a matter of regret. So I inquired who Doc Holliday was. I was informed that Doc was an old Griffin boy, the son of Major H.B. Holliday, who had lived in Griffin prior to the War Between the States.

"'Major Holliday had moved to Valdosta when his son was a small boy, but Doc Holliday (had later) returned to Griffin after the war and practiced dentistry here in an office in the old Merritt Building where Dr. Hopkins now is. While in Griffin, Doc Holliday developed tuberculosis, and went to Arizona, where he became famous – not as an outlaw, but as the relentless foe of the outlaws on that wild frontier. The description which my father gave of this singular person, (whom he

> *Historians and researchers have long debated the actual reason for his sudden departure from his Georgia homeland.*

> *Vestiges and memories of Doc Holliday remain strong in his Georgia homeland*

obviously had intimately known) established him in my imagination as a hero.'"

Sudden Departure

Following a diagnosis of the incurable and fatal disease within his lungs in late 1872, John Henry Holliday decided suddenly in January of 1873 to sell his half of the Merritt/Iron Front building, and by October of that year, records indicate he was practicing dentistry in faraway Dallas, Texas – the first stop "Doc" made in his countless western wanderings.

Historians and researchers have long debated the actual reason for his sudden departure from his Georgia homeland. Some sources have argued it was the tuberculosis with which he had been diagnosed – supposedly by his uncle, Dr. John Stiles Holliday – earlier that year. Others claim it was a star-crossed and ultimately shameful romance with his cousin, Mattie Holliday, which sent him wandering westward and her to a Convent for life.

Whatever the circumstances, vestiges and memories of Doc Holliday remain strong in his Georgia homeland. And visitors to the little second-floor office in Griffin's Iron Front building constantly imagine what it was like in the days of yesteryear, when a fearless Old West gunfighter was a simple dentist in a sleepy Southern town.

Leaving the "Old South" for the "Old West"

Though he was a native son of the old South, John Henry Holliday earned lasting fame in the old West in the 1880s.

He was born August 14, 1851, in Georgia's Spalding County in the small town of Griffin. In 1864, with the advancing threat of Gen. William Tecumseh Sherman's forces moving through Georgia during the U.S. Civil War, John Henry's father, Major Henry Burroughs Holliday, refugeed the family southward to Lowndes County where the 13-year-old youngster spent the remainder of his formative years, attending the Valdosta Institute and, upon graduation, leaving Georgia to attend the Pennsylvania College of Dental Surgery in Philadelphia. Following graduation from medical school and a return to Georgia for a short stint to practice dentistry in Griffin and Atlanta, "Doc" began a vagabond journey to the West, never again to return to Georgia.

The wandering Georgian traveled to and took up temporary residence in many towns of the old West. Places such as Dallas, Fort Griffin and Jacksboro, Texas; Pueblo, Leadville, Glenwood Springs and Denver, Colorado; Cheyenne, Wyoming; Deadwood, South Dakota (He reportedly was there when his friend, James Butler Hickok, was murdered); Dodge City, Kansas;

DODGE HOUSE – When John Henry arrived in Dodge City sometime around 1878, he took up residence in the Dodge House, a popular rooming facility in town. As with most Western burgs in those days of the old frontier, Dodge was a rough and tumble town full of cattle drovers and hard-nosed drifters, some of whom occasionally challenged Holliday until his reputation began preceding him.

LONGBRANCH SALOON – The Longbranch in Dodge City was nowhere near as impressive as the descriptions passed down in folklore and created by television westerns. Nevertheless, it was here that Doc, the Earp brothers, Bat Masterson, Bill Tilghman and other notables from the history of the old West passed many hours drinking, gambling and carousing in this former cow-town. (Courtesy of Kansas State Historical Society, Topeka, Kansas)

Mary Katherine "Big Nose Kate" Harony, Doc's consort during his days in the West, was photographed here circa 1869. Though ultimately bereft of any beauty and maligned in her later years, she was not unattractive as an adolescent. (Boyer Collection, Sharlot Hall Museum Archives)

Another view of the Dodge House, looking west down Front Street in Dodge City, Kansas. This photo was taken in 1874, just four years prior to Holliday's arrival in town. (Courtesy of Kansas State Historical Society, Topeka)

"Doc" Holliday had reached almost mythic proportions in the folklore of America, but it was not always so. After the initial newspaper coverage of the actual shoot-out behind the O.K. Corral in Tombstone in October of 1881, much of the fame of Wyatt Earp; his brothers James, Virgil, Morgan and Warren; and Doc Holliday, died out over the ensuing years. After the huge water pump at the Tombstone silver mines failed and the price of silver plummeted in the late 1880s, the town had withered and died, and the exploits of the Earps and Doc Holliday were almost completely forgotten.

Old Tombstone Today

By the 1890s in Tombstone, most of the miners had departed Cochise County (which included Tombstone). Since the town was located in the middle of the desert, most people just boarded up their homes or stores and left on horseback, in buckboards, and covered wagons. Most of them also simply abandoned in Tombstone most of their possessions which wouldn't fit into a covered wagon. Though Tombstone did get regular passenger train service on April 5, 1903, this was long after the good ol' days of the town had come and gone.

Las Vegas, New Mexico; Prescott, Tucson and Tombstone, Arizona; and numerous others all witnessed the comings and goings of the famous Georgian. Few towns held him or his interest more than two or three years.

Despite all these travels, it was the town of Tombstone, Arizona Territory which truly defined him. The years he spent in this fast-growing gold mining town in the desert – while he was still reasonably healthy – earned him the bulk of his lasting fame. And it was for these years that he is best remembered.

By the early 1990s – with the Hollywood releases of movies such as *Tombstone* (1993) starring Val Kilmer, Kurt Russell, and Sam Elliott – the name

HOLLIDAY SALOON – Las Vegas, New Mexico, was well-known as a haven for individuals with tuberculosis in the late 19th century. The town's main attraction was its hot springs located several miles northwest of the town plaza. In 1878, prior to taking up residence in Tombstone, Doc and Kate traveled to this town. Since they were residing in tandem, social mores required they identify themselves as "Dr. and Mrs. John H. Holliday," which they unhesitatingly did. In 1879, Doc, interestingly, built and opened a 17-foot by 30-foot one-story saloon here (hardly visible, but located just beyond the second telegraph pole on the left). This view looks west along Centre Street, and was taken circa 1880 or '81. (Courtesy of Museum of New Mexico)

As a result, Tombstone – despite the damage caused by two major fires – remained for many years much as Holliday and the Earps had left it. There really wasn't any way to steal or even freely take substantial quantities of the relics left in Tombstone. Few were willing to chance it across the desert.

The now-quiet, dusty, and virtual ghost-town lay dormant in this manner for well over half a century – until the 1950s when American servicemen at nearby Fort Huachuca began taking weekend excursions to the historic site.

A few years after arriving out West, Holliday had this full-length photograph taken in 1879 when he lived in Prescott, Arizona. At the time, he was rooming with the acting governor of Arizona Territory, John J. Gosper and Richard E. Elliott. (Photo courtesy of Craig Fouts)

MONTEZUMA STREET BOARD – Pictured is North Montezuma Street in Prescott in 1881. An 1879 Arizona Territory Census records Holliday's address as Montezuma Street where he, John J. Gosper, 39, and Richard E. Elliott, 45, were listed as rooming together. Elliott was known as a good friend of Virgil Earp, and Gosper, the acting governor of Arizona Territory. The boarding house at left in this photo was the one in which Holliday, Gosper and Elliott roomed. (Sharlot Hall Museum Archives, Prescott, AZ)

Though the streets are paved today and new buildings have filled in spots where older buildings had succumbed to neglect or one of the town's three major fires over the years, Allen (Main) Street in Tombstone is little-changed from the days of Doc Holliday and Wyatt Earp. A number of the original structures still stand. (Photo by Olin Jackson)

It was also about this same time that several writers – following the success of a nationally-broadcast Western television series based upon the life of Wyatt Earp – realized the value in publishing the biographies of the old West icons from this vicinity.

Luckily, the handful of local townspeople who remained in Tombstone – which had quite literally receded into virtual ghost-town status by the 1950s – eventually realized they had a money-maker on their hands. They banded together and created a historic district out of the town, preserving it for future generations – and for the income it could generate.

A number of the very structures which the Earps, Doc Holliday, Buckskin Frank Leslie, William Barclay "Bat" Masterson, Ike Clanton, Johnny Ringo, Texas John Slaughter, the McLaury

Wyatt Berry Stapp Earp was born 1848 and died in 1929. Doc Holliday saved Wyatt's life on at least one, and possibly two separate occasions, a fact that Wyatt never forgot. He and Doc, as a result, became life-long friends. They had parted in Tucson in 1879, when Wyatt – with several of his brothers – relocated to the booming silver-mining town of Tombstone. Doc departed Tucson for Tombstone in the autumn of 1880 where he and the Earps ultimately joined forces to defeat a group of semi-outlaws known as the Cow Boys.

Morgan Earp, younger brother of Wyatt, was born in 1851, the same year as Doc. The happy-go-lucky Morgan offered much more of a friendship to Holliday than did the dour Wyatt and Virgil, and the two spent considerable time in Tombstone drinking, carousing, and protecting each other in what was quickly becoming a very dangerous environment. Doc was particularly bereaved when Morgan was murdered in Campbell & Hatch Saloon in Tombstone in 1882. He ultimately sought vengeance - with Wyatt – upon Morgan's murderers. (Glenn G. Boyer Collection)

brothers, Turkey Creek Jack Johnson, Texas Jack Vermillion and a host of other famous and notorious figures of the old West had frequented, amazingly still stand even today in Tombstone.

Portions of the original O.K. Corral site have survived, though much of it was destroyed by the aforementioned fires. The original Wells-Fargo building also still exists, as does the billiard parlor (though re-built) in which Morgan Earp was murdered.

Though also heavily damaged by fire in 1882, the Crystal Palace Saloon was quickly rebuilt. It was here and in the Oriental Saloon which once existed across the street that Holliday, the Earps and most of the other aforementioned historic figures spent much time in the 1880s, gambling, drinking, fighting and carousing. The rebuilt Crystal Palace may still be visited today as well. Even the home once owned and inhabited by Virgil Earp on First Street still stands (as of this writing in 2023), as do the bank, and other structures.

The Birdcage Theatre is one of the more prominent relics from that day. Built in December of 1881, it was a popular place to enjoy bawdy women, gambling, theatrical productions, and other forms of adult entertainment in old Tombstone. It, amazingly, has been virtually completely preserved – with full furnishings – from the days when it was frequented by all the above-described historic figures – a virtual museum to the town's famed former inhabitants.

A Life In The West

John Henry Holliday was 21 in 1872, when he departed Georgia to begin his travels in the West. Interestingly, though doctors had advised that he had but a year or two left to live due to the tuberculosis in his lungs, he, in fact, lived for 15 more years, and in the interim, traveled throughout the last frontier in the continental United States, earning a well-deserved reputation as one of the deadliest gunmen walking the dusty streets of the old West.

Holliday has frequently been accused in print and folklore of being testy and irritable, but these likely were traits he acquired in his growing impatience with anyone unlucky enough to be perceived as wasting the Georgian's rapidly-diminishing time on this earth. It also didn't help matters that he liberally and regularly indulged in the "devil-water"

ORIENTAL SALOON – This corner site (above) was once occupied by the Oriental Saloon in which Wyatt Earp owned and operated a gambling concession in 1881, and in which Doc Holliday gambled and became embroiled in several gunfights that year. The Oriental was also the site of a vicious brawl between Holliday and saloon owner Milt Joyce in which Doc - always gamely-ready to defend himself despite his weakened condition - was beaten unconscious. In the street (left foreground), Tombstone Marshal Virgil Earp was shot and crippled for life in an assassination attempt on the evening of December 28, 1881, as he walked from the Oriental on his way to the Crystal Palace Saloon on the opposite side of the street. The Oriental Saloon was consumed by the Tombstone fire of 1882. (Photo by Olin Jackson)

BIRD CAGE THEATER – Though not built until December of 1881, this popular site of entertainment was patronized by most of the clientele of Tombstone, including Holliday and the Earps prior to their departure from the town. Today, the Bird Cage is one of the original structures still standing from the days of the Old West in Tombstone. After being boarded up and abandoned for 40+ years, the historic building was reopened as a tourist attraction in the 1960s, and still contains many of its original furnishings. (Photo by Olin Jackson)

of the West. In retrospect, who wouldn't have been short-tempered under these circumstances?

Holliday also was known to be very gracious to those who were courteous to him, and his honor was the most valuable asset he possessed. When bullied or persecuted as a result of his frail condition and appearance, Doc invariably proved to be a game opponent – and even seemed to welcome a good "knock-down, drag-out," even though he, more often than not, suffered the brunt of any injuries in these affairs. For that reason, he ultimately became quite adept in the use of firearms and knives for self-defense.

Though he often used what was known as a "pocket holster" (actually a reinforced pocket in his coat for carrying the heavy revolvers which dominated as weapons of that day), Doc Holliday was one of the first gunmen to use the new-fangled "shoulder holster." His weapon of choice early in his western career was an 1851 *Colt Navy* revolver given him by his uncle, one of four. Holliday later carried a nickel-plated .41 caliber *Colt Thunderer* which usually found refuge in his shoulder holster.

It has been documented in testimony from both Wyatt Earp and Bat Masterson that with these weapons, Doc Holliday was one of the deadliest shots

GOLDEN EAGLE BREWERY – Originally built in 1879 as the Golden Eagle Brewery, this saloon was burned in the devastating 1882 Tombstone fire, but was immediately rebuilt in the same spot and renamed the Crystal Palace Saloon. This was one of John Henry Holliday's favorite haunts in Tombstone. (Photo by Olin Jackson)

CRYSTAL PALACE SALOON – This view of Allen Street (looking west) in Tombstone was photographed in 1880. Despite being a silver-strike boomtown, the oppressive heat of Arizona kept the town's inhabitants off the streets during the height of each day. This view, at the intersection of 5th and Allen streets, shows the Eagle Brewery (right) with the Crystal Palace Saloon occupying the lower level of the building. This saloon was a favorite of Holliday's, and he spent many hours here drinking and gambling. Though this structure was partially burned in the fire of 1882, it was quickly rebuilt.

The interior of the Crystal Palace Saloon was photographed here in the 1880s. It was at these tables that John Henry Holliday spent much of his time gambling. This photograph, no doubt, was taken by the town's venerable photographer, Camillus S. Fly, in whose rooming house Doc Holliday took up quarters during his stay in Tombstone.

that they both had ever known. His considerable reputation for adeptness with weapons eventually began preceding him wherever his travels took him, earning him respect from bullies much larger and stronger than he who normally would have quickly overpowered him.

Despite his ill-luck in the contraction of tuberculosis, John Henry Holliday lived what might otherwise be called a charmed life. Although he was involved in quite a few gunfights and other affrays during his days in the old West, he managed to avoid death's door from these affairs, though he was wounded at least twice – once seriously. At the O.K. Corral gunfight in which he was credited with the death of at least one and possibly two of the opponents, a round from one of the McLaury revolvers grazed the pocket holster (in his coat) on his hip, causing him to suffer a bad bruise and a

limp for several days, but little else. Few other prominent gunmen of the old West – Earp and Masterson interestingly being two exceptions – endured this life without being killed. Wyatt Earp, amazingly, was never even wounded.

The now-famous shooting which actually occurred to the rear of the O.K. Corral in Tombstone, Arizona Territory on October 26, 1881 is very realistically portrayed in this illustration by Mark Warren. All the participants appear very nearly in the spots at which they stood when the shooting occurred. This incident, more than any other, galvanized public attention upon not only the Earp brothers, but John Henry "Doc" Holliday as well, earning them lasting fame in the annals of American history. Holliday appears in the street (center) holding the shotgun. The nearness of the participants in this illustration is quite accurate. (Illustration by Mark Warren)

Mannequins representing the participants in the O.K. Corral gunfight have been positioned in the approximate spot upon which each stood on October 26, 1881. Interestingly, John Henry Holliday is represented by the dark figure (far-right rear) with the shotgun near the entryway, and most historians place him on the opposite side of the Earps, near the street. The combatants also stood just a bit nearer to each other than is portrayed by the mannequins. At the time of the shoot-out, the area to the rear of the Earps and Holliday was completely open. The rear wall was added to the site to control ticket sales. (Photo by Olin Jackson)

All four of Wyatt's brothers were seriously wounded at some point in their lives, and two of them were killed in gunfire. His brother Morgan was assassinated in Tombstone in 1882, and Warren was murdered in 1900 in a barfight in Wilcox, Arizona, just a few miles away. *(Even though no one was arrested or charged in the incident, nor any inquest ever held, one can safely claim Warren was "murdered," since he was unarmed at the* time, and the .45 round fired at him was most intentional.)

James Butler "Wild Bill" Hickok was killed in Deadwood, South Dakota.

Frank McLaury was photographed prior to the O.K. Corral gunfight. Doc Holliday delivered one of the three fatal shots that killed McLaury in the famous shoot-out.

It is a documented fact that Doc Holliday delivered the gunshot that ended the life of Tom McLaury (pictured here). Tom and his brother Frank were never convicted of any crimes, and are believed by many to have been reasonably decent men for cattle thieves.

Johnny Ringo and most of the Clantons and McLaurys were killed in and around Tombstone in the 1880s. William "Billy the Kid" Bonney was killed in New Mexico in 1881. Jesse James, Pat Garrett, Butch Cassidy and the Sundance Kid, Billy Claiborne and many others all also met with equally bloody deaths at about this same time. Doc, Wyatt, and Masterson, however, seemed almost invulnerable to bullets, despite their lifestyles.

A Friendship With Earp

Doc and Wyatt had become fast friends in Dodge City, Kansas, while Wyatt was a deputy city marshal there. Holliday reportedly came to Wyatt's rescue (possibly saving his life) on two separate occasions – once in Dodge, and once again later in Tombstone – and Wyatt never forgot it. Though they quarreled in 1882 and went their separate ways, the two men nevertheless remained close friends to the end.

Wyatt was quoted as saying he enjoyed Doc's company because the clever dentist *"makes me laugh."* Doc was indeed known to have quite a sense of humor, as well as a love of practical jokes. According to one documented account, on one occasion when a stranger rode into Tombstone wearing a fancy suit and derby hat, Doc reportedly followed him throughout the town, gleefully tinkling a miniature sterling silver hand-held dinner bell everywhere the man went – much to the well-dressed gentleman's uncomfortable chagrin.

There is so much history in the little town of Tombstone, that one would be well-advised to spend at least a weekend in explorations there if ever a visit is made to this historic site. Above and beyond the commercial buildings and homes in the town associated with Holliday and the Earps, many other sites in

O.K. CORRAL VICTIMS – This photograph, one of the most famous in the Old West, almost certainly was taken by Camillus S. Fly, venerable photographer for many years in Tombstone, Arizona Territory. Pictured here are the victims of the shoot-out near the O.K. Corral: Frank McLaury, Billy Clanton, and Tom McLaury. Two of these fatalities were attributed to Doc Holliday.

BOOT HILL – The victims of the 1881 O.K. Corral gunfight were buried in "Boot Hill" Cemetery just outside Tombstone. Frank McLaury, Tom McLaury and Billy Clanton all went to the hereafter as a result of the brief but fierce 30-second shoot-out. (Photo by Olin Jackson)

that vicinity were often frequented by other individuals who later gained fame on the frontier.

The Earps had traveled to Tombstone specifically in search of gambling and gold mining opportunities. Holliday, too, made the arduous trip to this desert town which had not only become renowned for its gold and silver mines, but for the plethora of gambling opportunities as well. Indeed, he spent most of his years beyond his 21st birthday in search of the pleasures of life because, as a doctor, he was well aware of the premature aging and early death which accompanied the dreaded tuberculosis from which he suffered. He had watched in angst as his mother before him – whom he dearly loved – had suffered greatly from the same disease before finally succumbing to it.

Doc's adventures in Arizona Territory were many and varied. He was accompanied by his consort Katherine

CAMPBELL & HATCH ASSASSINATION – On March 18, 1882 at 10:00 P.M. Saturday night, Morgan Earp was assassinated (shot in the back) while playing billiards in Campbell and Hatch Saloon (photographed here shortly after the shooting) on Allen Street near the intersection of 5th Street in Tombstone. At the time that he was shot, Morgan was standing with his back to the rear of the saloon. A gunman fired thru one of the panes of the right-rear door (as one faces the rear of the room) for the kill-shot. The bullet entered Morgan's right side, shattered his spine and vital organs, and emerged from his left side. Doc Holliday, who was good friends with Morgan, took the news of his death extremely hard, and vowed to avenge him. He kept his word, helping Wyatt and Warren Earp hunt down the killers.

"Big-Nose Kate" Harony. The early days in Tombstone were a time of fun and delight for Holliday, but a criminal element composed of the Clantons, McLaurys, Johnny Ringo, and others eventually required the Earps – and thus also Doc – to take up arms against them.

Ultimately, in their last days in the Tombstone area in 1882, Doc, Wyatt Earp, Warren Earp, Texas Jack Vermillion, Turkey Creek Jack Johnson, Dan Tipton, and a handful of other close friends began what was known as *"the Vendetta Ride."* They in essence hunted down the outlaws who had assassinated one Earp (Morgan) and maimed another

(Virgil) for life and who had been protected for years by a corrupt judicial system in Cochise County. Months later, after much of the outlaw element had been "eliminated" (by what has been described by some as "vigilante justice"), Doc, Wyatt, and Warren began an odyssey across the West in a search for adventure and income opportunities.

Doc, with the remainder of the Vendetta cabal, drifted east to New Mexico Territory. At this point, the men reportedly separated. Turkey Creek Jack Johnson and Texas Jack Vermillion struck out on their own and faded into history. Eventually, Doc, Wyatt, Warren and

"Texas Jack" Vermillion was a renowned figure of the Old West of the 1880s, and a member of the "Vendetta Posse" who rode with Wyatt and Warren Earp, John Henry Holliday, "Turkey Creek" Jack Johnson, Sherman McMaster, and Dan Tipton, in pursuit of the "Cow Boy" outlaws of Arizona Territory in 1882. Vermillion was photographed here during his service as a Confederate soldier in the U.S. Civil War. Following the Vendetta Ride, Vermillion faded into history.

Tipton drifted northward up to Colorado, to the gold and silver mining towns which offered a better refuge from the Arizona authorities, and an opportunity for income from the gambling morass which always attended this industry.

John Henry traveled for a time with Wyatt and Warren before striking out on his own. The Earps – at least Wyatt – didn't mind camping out and sleeping upon the cold hard ground in the mountains of Colorado as they evaded Arizona law enforcement authorities, but John

Henry Holliday was accustomed to a bit more refinery, and his extreme illness reinforced this need for more hospitable circumstances. He therefore exchanged this "uncivil" life of camping and/or otherwise "roughing it in the mountains" for the bright lights and gambling mecca of Denver. The Earps and Tipton spent the summer of 1882 in Gunnison, with Doc traveling down from Denver to visit them there for a brief time.

For the rest of their days, both Doc and Wyatt did little more than travel and enjoy life. Neither of them ever owned a home after leaving Tombstone (Doc never owned a home at all, preferring to live in hotels and rooming houses his entire adult life), and they both literally went wherever the wind blew them.

The Lonely Years

In the ensuing years, John Henry Holliday essentially traveled alone. He had abandoned his female consort – "Big Nose" Katherine Harony – but continued to frequent the mining towns where quick money and poorly-schooled gamblers often offered steady income. The locations of these gold and silver-strike meccas invariably involved the extremes of nature – either the horrendous heat of the desert, or the freezing cold of the 12,000-foot Rocky Mountains. Each new extreme took its toll on the stamina of Doc Holliday.

The Georgian also was extremely limited by this point in his options for income. He now had such a reputation as "a lunger" that he was completely unable to ply his original trade as a dentist. Gambling in gold and silver-mining towns became his sole source of income. ...and it was a lonely preoccupation. He wasn't the only professional gambler on the circuit, so the "pickings" weren't always so easy.

GUNNISON, COLORADO HIDEAWAY – Following the "Vendetta Ride" with Wyatt and Warren Earp, Dan Tipton, "Turkey Creek" Jack Johnson, "Texas Jack" Vermillion, and Sherman McMaster, the men divided up and went their separate ways. Doc Holliday spent a few days with Wyatt, Warren and Tipton in Gunnison, Colorado, as the men eluded "law enforcement authorities" from Arizona in the summer of 1882. Though the weather was frigid and unforgiving, the Earps and their party preferred camping out in these climes, in order to put the odds in their favor should a bounty hunter attempt to seek them out. Doc, however, in his ill condition preferred the warmth, service, and finery of hotels, and soon departed Gunnison for Denver. Virginia Avenue in Gunnison – virtually unchanged from the days of Doc and Wyatt – was photographed here circa 1890s. (Denver Public Library, Western History Department)

Traveling from town to town and saloon to saloon, John Henry was able to maintain a reasonably steady income for several of the ensuing years, but with each new town, his physical appearance more and more became that of one who was weaker and weaker. This ultimately attracted a growing line-up of individuals suddenly willing to challenge the Georgian, hoping to earn the acclaim which would come with ending the life of the famed "Doc" Holliday.

And not only was he meeting new challengers, the fact that his travels were predominantly confined to gold and silver mining towns meant that he inevitably began meeting old enemies from his Tombstone days as well.

Confrontations In Colorado

He was well-educated, and, early in his life, seemed destined for a long productive career as a dentist. Fate, however, dealt him a different hand, sending him upon a circuitous route through the Old West where he faced many challenges before tuberculosis finally took him.

It was the wildlife and gold in the Rocky Mountains of the West which attracted the early miners and trappers as the last frontier in America was being settled in the 19th century. And with the gold-mining towns came other intrepid adventurers and gamblers such as John Henry Holliday.

Despite the many things that are known about him today, Holliday is, in many ways, an enigma – a mysterious individual. He traveled aimlessly throughout the West in the dying days of the old frontier. He left few writings of his experiences, so there are many gaps in his collective history. Newspaper accounts of that time were notoriously inaccurate and sometimes virtually fictitious, and many of the letters he sent back home to family and friends were later destroyed or lost.

It is known, however, that once out West, Doc had no intention of returning to his Georgia home. Whether this was due to his gambling and widely-reported gunfights, or to his debilitating health, is unknown today.

Despite their beauty, the Rockies in Colorado must have been very taxing for Doc toward the latter portion of the 1880s. His tortured lungs had been seriously impaired by the tuberculosis bacterium eating away within him. He must have been constantly out of breath, often wondering if he was going to make it to the next day. Anyone who has been to the 10-, 11-, and 12,000-foot altitudes in these mountains has experienced this gasping need for oxygen. One can only imagine how it affected an individual as sick as was John Henry Holliday.

By this point, however, the die had been cast. He had little left to live for, and no way to make a living except the gambling trade. His terrible coughing fits had eliminated any possibility of the pursuit of the dental profession for which he had been trained.

He spent a substantial amount of time in Denver from 1882-1884. His last days, however, were spent in the mining towns of Leadville and Glenwood Springs, Colorado.

From Arizona To Colorado

On the way to Denver, Colorado, in the summer of 1882, Doc reportedly had met up with several other old acquaintances in Pueblo: Bat Masterson, Sam Osgood and an individual known only as "Texas George." According to later reports, the men planned to attend the horse races in Denver and checked into the Windsor Hotel on the northeast corner of Eighteenth and Larimer streets in that city.

PALACE THEATER, DENVER – Of all the towns in the West, Doc preferred Denver, Colorado. Its comfortable and modern hotels, gambling establishments and opportunities for entertainment suited his nature. He traveled back and forth to Denver while living in nearby Leadville, and while on the run from corrupt Arizona authorities in the early- and mid-1880s who sought him for his involvement in the Vendetta Ride with the Earp faction. When in Denver, Doc frequented the Palace Theatre, as did Wyatt Earp and Bat Masterson. Masterson even managed it for a time.

The five-floor Windsor was a 300-room hotel – one of Denver's finest – and with its white marble floors, plush red carpeting and sixty-foot mahogany bar, it was just the type lavish establishment that the gambler from Georgia both admired and enjoyed. Again – the finer things in life always drew his attention.

One must find it at least mildly surprising that Masterson would stoop to socialize with Holliday at all, since it was widely-known that he detested him because of his oft-drunken and abrasive habits. One could also find Masterson's attitude toward Holliday ironic, since Masterson himself would soon be officially ejected from Denver and told never to return due to his own outrageous drunken behavior.

Unfortunately, Doc's penchant for trouble caught up with him once again

in Denver. An individual by the name of Perry Mallen arrested Holliday on a warrantless and fraudulent murder charge associated with Doc's days in Arizona Territory. Mallen identified himself as an associate and envoy of Sheriff Johnny Behan of Cochise County in Arizona, where Doc was in fact *"Wanted"* for his participation in the earlier-referenced *"Vendetta Ride."*

As a result, Mallen was able to have Doc jailed in Colorado, but the Georgian ultimately was rescued several weeks later by Bat Masterson, who, as a law enforcement official himself, indicated he was taking Doc into his custody for the return to Arizona. Masterson escorted Doc out of town and then set him free. Though he generally found Holliday detestable, he came to the tubercular gambler's assistance at the request of his friend Wyatt Earp, who had come to his (Bat's) aid on more than one occasion in the past.

Denver To Leadville

In a continued effort to escape his past, and to maintain his livelihood in gambling, Doc departed Denver and traveled by stage approximately 125 miles southwestward to the town of Leadville in Colorado. This community had been a mining boomtown since 1877 when a rich vein of silver and lead ores had been discovered. By the time Doc arrived in July of 1882, the mining of these metals had slowed, but there were still many gambling opportunities at the scores of saloons and bordellos yet remaining in this former boomtown.

One can only guess today at Holliday's perception of Leadville back in the 1880s. Did he enjoy the snow, or did he simply find it to be another shivering impediment to life? What was it like in the bleak shadows of the Rockies in a time when there was no indoor plumbing in most establishments, and no warm comfortable automobiles in which to travel about? Granted there were trains to the site. The *Denver & Rio Grande* had arrived in 1880, and the *Colorado Midland* arrived in 1887. Doc reportedly made use of them whenever possible, but more often than not, he either traveled on horseback or within the freezing confines of a jarring stagecoach.

When he arrived in the high mountain town, Doc found employment as a faro dealer at Cyrus "Cy" Allen's Monarch Saloon which was located at 320 Harrison Avenue. *(This structure still exists today in this now sparsely-populated town.)* However, he didn't last long there. His illness had caused him to become heavily dependent upon alcohol by this time, and it affected his ability to perform his job. His employment at

John Henry Holliday as he appeared during the so-called "Vendetta Ride." Gone was the vitality of youth even though he was only in his thirties, age-wise. (Photo courtesy of the Colorado Historical Society)

Allen's Saloon ended almost as quickly as it had begun.

According to reports, Holliday found new work nearby as a faro dealer in one of the clubrooms of Hyman's Saloon owned by Mannie Hyman. It was located at 316 Harrison Avenue next door to the Tabor Opera House *[both of which also are still in existence as of this writing (2023) in downtown Leadville].* Doc apparently decided this was a good spot to put down some roots. He was able to obtain a room upstairs on the northwest corner of this building. *(At last check, this room was still being maintained as a historic memorial to the famous gambler.)*

Bleak Existence

Doc's tiny room – seven by fourteen feet – was his refuge in these years in Leadville. It gave him a beautiful – albeit bleak no doubt to him – view of the snow-covered Rockies. When he wasn't sleeping, Doc almost always could be found in Hyman's saloon, dealing the faro games, or, across the street at John G. Morgan's Board of Trade Saloon *[present-day Silver Dollar Saloon which also still stands as of this writing (2023)]* where he often sat on the player's side of the table, playing stud poker.

According to reports, during the years 1882 to 1886, Doc occasionally visited most of the gambling houses along Harrison Street, plying his trade. However, by this time, his physical condition had severely debilitated his skills as a gambler, and his winnings had declined considerably. He also almost certainly had difficulty finding a table at which to play due to his bad cough. As a result, he was often short of money, and began leaning upon the goodwill of others to survive.

It seems almost pitiful to imagine Doc Holliday by this point in his life. He was very quickly succumbing to the tuberculosis ravaging his lungs and his health in general. He had always been slight in stature, but had been lightning quick with strong hands and arms, and usually capable of handling himself when confronted. His growing alcoholism, however, had affected his diet – and thus his weight and strength. He had also lost most of his stamina due to the tuberculosis in his lungs and to two bouts of pneumonia with which he suffered during this period. In short, Doc Holliday was a pitiful sight by the mid-1880s.

When the whiskey – with which Doc was liberally self-medicating himself – ceased to offer a balm to the pain and destruction of his lungs, the once handsome dentist and gambler reportedly found another medication – laudanum. A local druggist who owned an apothecary at the corner of Sixth and Harrison streets, befriended Holliday and reportedly provided the drug to him.

His growing dependency on laudanum coupled with the severe bouts of pneumonia weakened Holliday even more. He was able to sustain himself with an occasional win at the card tables, but it was a meager existence at best.

Becoming A Target

As a result of his obviously weak physical state, the wolves began circling Holliday. He increasingly became a target for roughneck gamblers and predators in general who sought to earn a name for themselves by becoming the person who out-gunned or defeated the great Doc Holliday.

In his prime, Doc had usually needed only to identify himself to most belligerents – even vicious ones – in order to avoid a fight. However, by the time he reached Leadville, he was so obviously weak and debilitated that he had become a regular target of gunmen and outlaws. More and more, the stronger bullies pushed ever harder to humiliate Holliday and goad him into a fist or gunfight.

Though he was weak and disabled, Doc – to his credit – was never a coward, and he would not be bullied, regardless of the circumstances. For this reason, Leadville, Colorado, enjoys the unique distinction of being the site of John Henry Holliday's last gunfight.

Two of Doc's old Tombstone, Arizona, enemies – William "Billy" Allen and Johnny Tyler – unfortunately were living in Leadville at the time of Doc's residence there. According to Karen Holliday Tanner in **Doc Holliday: A Family Portrait**, Allen was a former Leadville policeman who had been a friend of Ike Clanton – Doc's old Tombstone nemesis. Allen had even served as a prosecution witness during the O.K. Corral shooting inquest and had testified against Doc.

"... *he (Allen) had accompanied Reuben Coleman on the day of the gunfight in Tombstone*," Ms. Tanner writes. "*They had walked down Allen Street through the O.K. Corral to the front of Camillus S. Fly's Gallery (behind Fly's Boarding House). It was believed by some, and certainly by Doc, that during the fracas, Allen had fired a number of shots aimed at both Holliday and the Earps from the passageway between Fly's buildings. After coming to Leadville, Allen had been a part-time policeman and had been hired as a bartender at the Monarch Saloon.*"

Confronting Johnny Tyler

Ms. Tanner also explains how Johnny Tyler – after the Tombstone years – was dealing faro at the Casino Gambling Hall in Leadville. "*Tyler had not forgotten the humiliation he had suffered in 1880 when he was evicted from Tombstone's Oriental Saloon by Wyatt Earp with Doc looking on, laughing and taunting him,*" Ms. Tanner adds. "*Tyler harbored tremendous anger and resentment toward Doc and now prepared to vent it.*

"*Johnny Tyler and Billy Allen plotted their vendetta. . . In August of 1884, Doc found himself in the unenviable position of owing Billy Allen five dollars. Allen, knowing of Doc's dire straits (financially), had willingly loaned the money, assuming that Doc would have difficulty repaying the debt. This would give Allen justification to goad the weak, sick Holliday into a gunfight. Doc had borrowed the money with the promise to repay it in less than a week. Seven days later, he had to go to Billy and humbly explain that he had not been able to collect an outstanding debt and therefore did not have the money (to repay Allen).*"

For a number of weeks in Leadville,

William J. "Billy" Allen was photographed circa 1895, in Carrollton, Missouri, approximately 11 years after being wounded by Holliday in Leadville. In this photo, to even the least discriminating eye, Allen looked every bit the part of the bullying predator described in historic accounts. He had blithely assumed he would severely beat, if not kill, the sick and weakened Holliday in a confrontation, but he was seriously disappointed, and, in actuality, lucky to have survived the incident. By that point, other than his immortal soul, Holliday had absolutely nothing left to lose, and fully intended – if possible – to arrange the meeting between Allen and his Maker. Though he survived, Allen never again confronted Holliday.

Doc was continuously insulted and humiliated by Johnny Tyler and his cohorts. In an earlier day, they would not have dared to confront and challenge him in such a manner, but in 1884, Doc was only a shadow of his former persona, and his antagonizers knew it. They relentlessly taunted him, threatening him with gunplay.

By this time, Doc no longer even carried a gun, having been threatened with jail-time should he be caught with a

FINAL GUNFIGHT – During the winter of 1883-84, Doc Holliday found work at Mannie Hyman's Saloon at 316 Harrison in Leadville. It was here on the afternoon of August 19, 1884, that he confronted the predator Billy Allen, wounding him severely with a Colt's .41 revolver as Allen moved aggressively through the doorway of the saloon in pursuit of the sick Georgian. This was the final gunfight in which Doc Holliday was ever involved. (Courtesy of Denver Public Library)

MANNIE HYMAN'S SALOON – John Henry Holliday lived upstairs on the second floor in this building. The window of his room is visible (above, left) at the corner. A saloon which once existed downstairs was the site at which he confronted Billy Allen. (Photo by Olin Jackson)

sidearm. He was virtually destitute, and since he could not afford to pay a fine for possession of a firearm nor survive in the cold dank jails of that day, he had sworn off his weapons entirely. After having been stopped and searched a number of times by the Leadville police, he was very careful not to violate the city ordinance concerning firearms.

"Words passed between him and Tyler and his cronies at Hyman's Bar, and several of them called him to 'pull his gun,'" a local Leadville newspaper reporter wrote at the time. *"He said he had none, and as he passed outside, he was called filthy names. . . Next day, he told* this writer, with tears of rage coming to his eyes as he talked, that they were insulting and humiliating him because they knew he could not retaliate."*

Allen Eats Lead

Billy Allen, who had been waiting for his opportunity, finally issued Doc an ultimatum: Pay the debt owed to him by noon of the following Tuesday or face the threat of severe violence.

"When Tuesday arrived, some of Doc's friends went to his room and told him that Allen was looking for him with a gun," Ms. Tanner continued. *". . . . On the stairway down into the saloon, Doc asked Mannie Hyman to get an officer for protection. He continued into the saloon but did*

The front portion of the room occupied in 1884 by Mannie Hyman's Saloon was a gift shop at the time this photo was snapped almost 120 years later. It was on this spot that Doc Holliday worked and confronted Billy Allen. At that time, a bar existed along the wall to the right, and Holliday was positioned just behind it near the front window. After threatening Holliday, Allen entered the doorway which at that time existed where the gift items framed in the big picture window (left center) exist in this photo. (Photo by Olin Jackson)

not find Allen. He asked his friend and fellow boarder Frank Lomeister, who was working the day shift as bartender, to get Capt. Edmond Bradbury of the Leadville Police Department or Marshal Harvey Faucett, adding that he did not want to sit around for the afternoon unprotected."

Though death's angels were closing in upon him, John Henry Holliday continued to fight for life. According to reports of this famous incident, he returned to his room where he remained in the tiny enclosure until approximately five o'clock in the afternoon. He knew, however, that he eventually would have to go back down to the saloon to work, but he also knew that he would have to defend himself if he did, and that he couldn't afford the fine nor a prison term if he was caught with a firearm.

Totally desperate by this point, Doc instructed one of his friends to take his (Doc's) Colt's .41 revolver down and hide it behind the bar. He then went down to the saloon himself and sat near the end of the bar behind the cigar case where he could quickly grab his gun if necessary.

It was obviously a very dramatic setting, one more characteristic of Doc's earlier days perhaps in Dodge City or Tombstone. According to reports of the incident, Billy Allen eventually did enter the saloon, and he had the misfortune to have his hand in his pocket as if holding a weapon.

When Doc saw Allen's hand in his gun pocket, that posture created Doc's alibi to defend himself. Without hesitation – and in a flashback to the days when he fearlessly defended himself – Doc Holliday immediately grabbed his handgun and quickly fired a round at Allen. The bullet found its mark, striking the unfortunate victim in the fleshy part of his upper arm and severing an artery.

When Allen fell to the floor in pain, Doc fired at him yet again. He meant to legally end this threat once and for all, because he knew if he did not, Allen would be back to try yet again. This second round struck the door sill, barely missing Allen's head. Even with his severe debilitation, Doc was still a deadly-accurate gunman if necessary.

Before he could get off another shot, however, Doc was grabbed from behind by Henry Kellerman who wrestled the gun away. This action almost certainly saved Billy Allen's miserable life, and also possibly saved Doc from being charged with first degree murder.

Doc, nevertheless, was subsequently arrested by the Leadville marshal and charged with *"Assault with intent to commit murder."* He was locked up in jail and his bail reportedly was set at $5,000.00 – both circumstances were exactly what the gambler had feared. In 1883, the sum of $5,000.00 was the equivalent of well over $150,000.00 in 2023 dollars.

Interestingly, in an earlier day and time, John Henry Holliday might possibly have raised that amount to bail himself out of jail, but by the time of his days in Leadville, the ex-dentist – as explained above – was living virtually hand-to-mouth. For that reason, $5,000.00 was

> *Doc Holliday immediately grabbed his handgun and quickly fired a round at Allen.*

an impossibly high bail for him to raise, and he must surely have thought he was going to be incarcerated in a freezing-cold and damp jail for months until his trial date arrived.

On Trial For Assault

Interestingly, though it has seldom been publicized, Doc – despite his oft-abrasive personality – seemed to consistently cultivate a coterie of close friends willing to help him when necessary. Two of these stepped forward immediately. John G. Morgan and Samuel Houston, co-owners of the Board of Trade Saloon *(which also still exists today in Leadville as of this writing in 2023)* arrived the next morning and immediately posted bail for Doc.

In the trial that followed, a number of eye-witnesses testified to the threats that had been issued at Doc by Allen, and the circumstances of the shooting that had followed. Doc took the stand on his own behalf and explained the details of the loan and the subsequent threats.

"I saw Allen coming in with his hand in his pocket, and I thought my life was as good to me as his was to him," Holliday explained in his courtroom testimony. *"I fired the shot and he fell on the floor, and (I) fired the second shot; I knew that I would be a child in his hands if he got hold of me; I weigh 122 pounds; I think Allen weighs 170; I have had pneumonia three or four times. I don't think I would have been able to protect myself against him."*

The jury ultimately returned a verdict of "Not Guilty" in the case of People vs John Henry Holliday. Following this last gunfight, the curtain essentially came down on the public life of John Henry Holliday, ending his gun-fighting days forever. He was never again involved in a shooting incident.

Not too long after the trial, Doc, for good reason, no doubt felt the urge to move on to another town. He first took a short trip back to Denver one last time before returning briefly to Leadville.

Holliday had learned of a town called Glenwood Springs, Colorado, which had a variety of steamy sulfur water grottos outside town, and of the fact that some individuals had gone there for the treatment of various health problems. This town, no doubt, was doubly attractive, since it was not only known as a health resort, but also as a mining town too, with many saloons and other gaming establishments which offered Doc yet another opportunity to ply the gambling trade. It offered just the opportunity he sought at this point in his life.

Last Days In Glenwood

Today, Glenwood Springs isn't much larger than it was in Doc's day in 1887. (It might even be smaller.) The warm springs are still active and frequented by many individuals interested in the presumed curative qualities of the waters.

Doc once again found himself on a cold, bumpy, and exceedingly uncomfortable stagecoach headed farther up into the Colorado Rockies. He made the

By 1887, Doc's appearance reportedly was that of an individual well-advanced in years

trip from Leadville to Glenwood Springs in May of 1887. [The railroad (Denver & Rio Grande) did not reach Glenwood Springs until October 5, 1887, so it was unavailable as a travel medium for Doc's trip.]

By 1887, Doc's appearance reportedly was that of an individual well-advanced in years, with silver hair and an emaciated stooped posture. According to a news article of that day, "He walked down the street with a feeble tread and a downcast look. If he heard a (gun)shot, he raised his head with eager attention and glanced this way and that." Even in 1887, Glenwood Springs obviously was still somewhat wild and unsettled.

He fully intended – and did – take advantage of the sulfur springs in a never-ending quest to stem the tide of the destructive bacteria in his lungs. Ironically, rather than curing Doc's ills, the acidic and acrid vapors caused even more damage to his already-ruined system. His cough quickly worsened, and his health declined even more rapidly.

Just as had been the case in both Denver and Leadville, Doc reportedly was admired and welcomed by a number of individuals, and quickly cultivated a coterie of friends in Glenwood Springs in the weeks immediately following his arrival.

After settling into his new quarters, he reportedly attempted once again to ply his old trade at the gambling tables. By this point, however, he simply no longer had the stamina to participate. Gone was the vitality which had served him so well in Kansas and Arizona and earlier

Mary Katherine Harony Cummings ("Big-Nosed Kate") was photographed here circa 1890. Gone was the limited beauty she had enjoyed as a young adult, but her devotion and attendance to John Henry Holliday in his final hours was still strong and commendable. (A.W. Bork and Glenn G. Boyer Collection)

in Colorado. With the departure of his strength also went his will to live. He no doubt knew his last days truly were upon him at this point.

His spirits understandably were low, and, according to Karen Holliday Tanner, Doc had written to his former consort – Mary Katherine "Big-Nose Kate" Harony in Globe, Arizona – telling her he was traveling to Glenwood Springs, and asking her to join him there. By this point, Doc must have known he was fast approaching the time when he would need someone to physically assist him with the rudimentary tasks of daily life. He no doubt knew of no one to call upon except Kate, and she, to her credit, responded admirably.

Doc and Kate had traveled many miles together earlier in their lives. They had enjoyed many adventures across the West in places like Las Vegas, New Mexico; Dodge City, Kansas; Tucson and Tombstone, Arizona. This bond no doubt held them together as Doc fought for breath in the final months of his life.

In Kate's Care

Many accounts today indicate Doc died alone and abandoned in the Hotel Glenwood in his last days. One recently-discovered (2004) and very credibly-documented record *(explained in detail in the following chapter)* however, indicates an entirely different scenario.

Whatever the circumstances, Doc took a room at the Hotel Glenwood on the northeast corner of Grand Avenue and Eighth Street in Glenwood Springs. This exceptional hotel had just recently been built (1886), and was among the finest in the West at that time. It offered among its amenities electric lights, both hot and cold running water in every room, and even flush-toilets. The water was pumped directly from the Grand (later renamed Colorado) River, since there was no water system in the town, with the sewage being returned directly into the river downstream.

Most of the old saloons and gambling establishments in Glenwood Springs are gone today, replaced by more modern structures. The Hotel Glenwood burned to the ground on December 14, 1945, killing five people, and destroying forever the final home of John Henry Holliday.

Though the town fathers of Glenwood Springs seem to have paid limited heed toward historic preservation over the years, the community yet retains a scenic air, unique with its warm springs. The stark Rockies are still startlingly beautiful, but they must have been cold and forbidding to Doc in his dying days.

Photographed sometime after 1898 during one of the "Strawberry Days" parades in Glenwood Springs, Colorado, this funeral coach from 1885 quite likely transported Holliday's body to the vicinity of Linwood Cemetery on November 8, 1887. (Courtesy of Frontier Historical Society)

During the last 57 days of his life, John Henry Holliday reportedly rose from his bed at the Hotel Glenwood only twice. He and Kate reportedly relied upon the bellhop to serve them their meals so that Kate did not have to leave his bedside.

It is poignant to imagine Kate attending to him in these last hours. She easily could have ignored his request to join him in Colorado, knowing the task of caring for him during this time would not be pleasant. She reportedly never wavered from her duties however, and even used her meager savings to support them after Doc could no longer work. In her later years, she said she considered her relationship with Doc to be a marriage.

All the years of smoking, drinking, poor diet and poor care finally caught up with the famed gambler. Pneumonia and tuberculosis ultimately combined to do what many gunmen over the years had failed to accomplish. By the third week in October of 1887, Doc was delirious, and by Monday of November 7, he reportedly was unable to speak, so many researchers and writers maintain it is unlikely he ever uttered the now-famous last words, "This is funny," as claimed in folklore. He died on November 8, 1887.

Kate's Last Days

Interestingly, Doc's consort for all those years in Arizona and Colorado – Mary Katherine Horony – reportedly gathered up Doc's belongings from his room after his death, and shipped them to Doc's one true love – his cousin, Sister Mary Melanie of the Order of the Sisters of Mercy – who had entered a convent to become a nun after Doc left Atlanta, Georgia for the West.

After she had disposed of Doc's last possessions, Kate then left the sadness in Glenwood Springs forever, but reportedly remained for a time at her brother's home nearby in the Crystal Valley region of Colorado. On March 2, 1890,

Alexander Harony, brother to Kate ("Big Nose") Harony (a.k.a. "Haroney"), lived with his family at Penny Hot Springs in the Crystal Valley near Aspen, Colorado. Following her final duties with Doc in Glenwood Springs, Kate (second from right) visited with her brother for a short time. (Glenn G. Boyer Collection)

she married George M. Cummings in the mining town of Aspen, Colorado, a well-known ski resort today. The couple moved about the West before finally settling in Bisbee, Cochise County, Arizona, in 1895, just a few miles from Tombstone where Doc had gained so much fame in 1881-1882.

This marriage lasted approximately nine years before Kate left Mr. Cummings who was an alcoholic. *(Katherine Harony enjoyed little if any luck in her selection of men.)* On June 2, 1900, she accepted employment as the housekeeper of John J. Howard of Dos Cabezas, Arizona. She remained in his employ until Howard's death in 1930. On June 13, 1931, Kate wrote to Arizona Governor George W. Hunt requesting permission to live in the state-supported Arizona Pioneers Home in Prescott.

Governor Hunt reportedly granted Kate's request. For the last nine years of her life, Mary Katherine Cummings (nee Horony) – also known in history as "Big-Nose Kate" – lived out her final days in the town where, in 1880, she and Doc had spent time together just prior to his Tombstone days. She died on November 2, 1940, and was buried at the Pioneer Cemetery in Prescott.

Today, one can only imagine how John Henry Holliday felt in his last days, separated from his family and friends back in Georgia, as well as his surrogate family – the Earps – who, by that time, were scattered from Arizona to California. Thankfully, he did have Kate in his last days. She no doubt brought him comfort in his final hours.

It, however, seems a pity the last remains of one of the most famous and fabled of all the individuals of the old West, lie in an unknown and unmarked grave today, mysterious and yet respected even in death. Ironically, that's probably just the way Doc would have wanted it. His lonely wandering soul is finally at peace.

Retracing Doc's Footsteps in the Colorado Rockies

Today, many of Holliday's former haunts on the frontier of the Old West in the 1880s surprisingly still exist, much as they did when he yet breathed the fresh Colorado air.

Looking for a great vacation opportunity with lots of Old West history? Knowing that many of the historic sites from the 1880s still exist out West, I made a special effort to visit as many of them as possible before time, the elements, and "progress" team up to erase them forever. I also wanted to see the last towns in the old West in which Holliday had lived during the years prior to his death in 1887.

Today, almost all serious researchers and historians know that John Henry Holliday was born in Griffin, Georgia, where he spent the first thirteen years of his life, and that he spent the remainder of his formative years at the family's Civil War-era home in Valdosta, Georgia, to which they relocated in 1864 to escape the ravages of Gen. William T. Sherman's Union Army. I wanted to retrace the route Holliday had taken in the final years of his life after he had moved to the West and prior to his expiration from the ills of tuberculosis in Glenwood Springs, Colorado in 1887.

An Arduous Journey

Driving the hundreds of desolate miles across Kansas, I couldn't help but imagine what it must have been like for Holliday – sick as he was – to travel by stagecoach and on horseback to various towns in this state in the 1870s and 1880s. He traveled by train when possible, but since railroads in the West were somewhat limited at that time, he took stagecoaches to most of his destinations and traveled by horseback in some of the more remote areas.

I'm not certain how Doc originally traveled to Denver. He visited it a number of times both early in his career out West and in the years just prior to his death simply because it was a more modern and civilized city than most any other in the West at that time. He supported himself by gambling, and Denver, as a result of its gold rush heritage, offered many saloons and gambling houses at which the former dentist could ply his trade.

By the time he returned to Denver in 1882, however, he was a *"Wanted"* man in Arizona for his involvement in what came to be known as *"the Vendetta Ride."* He had joined Wyatt and Warren Earp, Turkey Creek Jack Johnson, Texas Jack Vermilion, Sherman McMaster, Dan Tipton and several others in hunting down the outlaws – particularly those known as the "Cow Boys" who had been involved in the murder of Morgan Earp in Tombstone, Arizona.

As a result, Denver no longer was able to offer John Henry the comfortable refuge he had enjoyed in the past. After being arrested there and very nearly extradited back to Arizona, he was literally forced to leave the town and to seek new horizons. He therefore moved on to other gold mining towns which also offered gambling opportunities.

Today, few if any of Doc's former haunts in Denver remain for the curious. Modern development has eliminated virtually all of the old hotels and saloons from yesteryear in this town. I decided not to waste my time searching for remnants of his days in that city.

Better Luck In Leadville

One needs only to travel the highlands of Colorado today in a comfortable automobile to understand just how uncomfortable it must have been riding in a freezing cold jarring stagecoach for hundreds of miles through the dangerous snow-covered Rocky Mountains of the 1880s. Warm comfortable restrooms at various locations and hot meals at safe comfortable restaurants were of course non-existent.

In the stage coach inns – known as "stands" in those days – where the stage overnighted, male travelers slept several to a bed – oftentimes just to stay warm – and that is assuming there were beds, which many times there were not. Holliday, however, just as most other travelers of that day and time, was a resilient individual, but his illness coupled with the harshness of the trip took a toll upon his health.

According to records, the tubercular

I wanted to visit this historic high-altitude town to see what vestiges of Holliday remain there today.

dentist took a stage to Leadville in 1882, living there for four years (the most time he spent in any spot in the West). I wanted to visit this historic high-altitude town to see what vestiges of Holliday remain there today.

To reach this isolated little burg, I drove Interstate 70 *(which I had followed all the way across Kansas and eastern Colorado the previous two days)* and took the Copper Mountain/Leadville exit some miles west of Denver. There, I soon found myself on a precipitous climb up into the mountains – *very* precipitous.

After driving for many miles with virtually no road signs whatsoever, I eventually reached the town which, as a result of its many gambling opportunities, had attracted Holliday's attention in 1882. My usually calm wife was working on "my last good nerve" (as if the dangerous drive hadn't been bad enough), because she was convinced we were lost and headed in the wrong direction. I have many faults, but a lack of a sense of direction is not one of them. When we emerged from the mountains into the outskirts of Leadville at approximately 8:30 p.m. that evening, it was a relief to her *and me*, to say the least.

Located at 10,152 feet above sea level, this Old West mining town is surrounded by Colorado's tallest peaks, and includes many historic aspects above and beyond the distinction of being one of Holliday's former residences. We entered the town on historic Harrison Avenue, enjoying almost the identical view as had Holliday over 100 years earlier.

HARRISON AVE, 1880 – Photographed here shortly before the arrival of Doc Holliday in town, Leadville is just beginning to experience a bit of upgraded development. Notice the concrete sidewalks which have recently been constructed. The street, however, remains a dirt conveyance, and much of the town's early rustic status is yet visible.

HARRISON AVE IN MODERN TIMES – Photographed in 2001, this main thoroughfare – though now crowded with additional civic structures – still appears much as it did during the days of the Old West. Doc lived in a room above Hyman's Saloon at 316 Harrison Ave, which still stands today approximately two-thirds of the way down this street on the left. (Photo by Olin Jackson)

The historic Tabor Opera House which still stands in town on Harrison hosted many famous entertainers and celebrities over the years, including boxer Jack Dempsey, author Oscar Wilde, magician Harry Houdini and even musician John Philip Sousa and his Marine Band.

The Tabor home at 116 E. 5th Street in town was built by H.A.W. ("Haw" Horace) Tabor sometime around 1877. Horace and his first wife, Augusta, lived in this residence until 1881. At that time, Horace moved to the nearby Windsor Hotel to be near his mistress "Baby Doe." The Tabor love triangle grew into a national scandal, ultimately ending in a divorce between Horace and Augusta, and a marriage between Horace and Baby Doe.

Unfortunately, Tabor, who was extremely wealthy, was heavily invested in silver. In 1893, after the repeal of the *Sherman Silver Act* which removed silver as the metal which "backed" currency issued in the United States, a silver

LEADVILLE – Photographed from Carbonate Hill, this view of Leadville was taken circa 1884 at the time Doc Holliday lived in the town. At this time, silver was yet being widely-mined in the boom-town, as is indicated by the dense civic development. (Photo courtesy of Denver Public Library Western Collection)

panic ensued, sending silver prices plummeting. Tabor, who had owned the huge Tabor Grand Building and the opulent Tabor Opera House among other properties, began a long but steady slide toward insolvency.

In 1895, Horace Tabor, amazingly, finally did declare bankruptcy, and Baby Doe eventually began walking the streets of Leadville in rags. Also in 1895, Augusta Tabor died as a result of respiratory problems. She, interestingly, was a millionaire at her death. Horace had become a pauper.

In 1884, in the building next door to the Tabor Opera House, John Henry Holliday was involved in his last gunfight. I had read about Leadville and Holliday's gunfight there, and attempted to visit the town on a previous trip to Colorado in December of 1998. An unexpected heavy snowfall, and the subsequent closure of the roads into the town,

however, ultimately prevented me from accomplishing that objective.

In the 1880s, Leadville was a gold and silver mining town of considerable proportions. Holliday had turned to gambling – which had served him well in places like Dodge City, Kansas; Tombstone Arizona; and Denver, Colorado – as a profession. Leadville offered a continuation of the same gambling opportunities.

Historic But "Spartan"

As a result of the extreme elevation of Leadville – even with my healthy lungs – I quite often felt the effects of the oxygen-depleted air. I could only imagine that Holliday, with his ruined lungs, must have struggled to an unbelievable degree. He is known to have contracted pneumonia several times while living here, but amazingly survived the illness each time.

GOLD MINES – Despite the intoxicating beauty of the soaring Rockies in the distance, Leadville, Colorado, can impose a challenge to even the most-hardy of travelers. This, however, did not deter the thousands of fortune-seekers who flocked to this locale in the 1870s after gold and silver were discovered on the slopes above town. This view, photographed from the area of many of the gold mines, looks back toward the community. (Photo by Olin Jackson).

TABOR OPERA HOUSE - Located next door to the now-aged Hyman Saloon building where Holliday lived and worked, the Tabor, which opened in 1879, was said to be the grandest theater in its day between St. Louis and San Francisco. Wealthy businessman and silver magnate H.A.W. "Haw" Tabor built the structure which seated 880 people within its once-luxurious interior. It hosted many notables during Leadville's heydays, including appearances by heavyweight boxing champion Jack Dempsey, author Oscar Wilde, famed magician Harry Houdini, and renowned musician John Philip Sousa and his Marine Band. Holliday, who thoroughly enjoyed theatrical productions, no doubt, visited this facility at least occasionally from 1882 to 1886. (Photo by Olin Jackson)

In 1884, the population of Leadville was approximately 20,000 (not counting "soiled doves" as the towns literature proclaims). According to records, it had 92 saloons, 61 lawyers, numerous gambling houses and brothels, and 8 churches. A number of these same buildings still exist today, and the entire town retains a somewhat "frontier" appearance.

My accommodations for the next few days in Leadville would be at the historic Delaware Hotel in the heart of the town. The Delaware has reigned as an architectural cornerstone of Leadville's *National Historic District* for years, and is often referred to as the "Crown Jewel" of the town. According to this interesting inn's literature, it has played host to a number of notables over the years, including even outlaw Butch Cassidy himself, who reportedly once roomed in the hostelry during one notorious visit to the town.

As with Tombstone, Arizona,

Leadville, Colorado – due to its somewhat isolated and inhospitable location – has changed little from the Old West days of Holliday. There has been very little "modern development" over the years. Some of the buildings from yesteryear have disappeared as a result of fire and general neglect, and occasionally, a new church or a new saloon – designed much the same as the old ones – has been built, but little else has changed. The area presumably is simply too unattractive, geographically, to experience any significant increase in population.

To understand this, all one has to do is walk to a second or third floor room in a hotel in the town. Following this effort, a full four or five-minute recuperation will be required by almost anyone over 35 who has not lived in the area for a period of time and become accustomed to the paucity of oxygen.

For this reason, I hereby offer the following advice to future travelers to this site: The Delaware Hotel has three stories of rooms – but there is no elevator in the facility. *Therefore, reserve your room in advance – and get a room on the first floor*. Otherwise, you will have no one to blame but yourself for your sufferings as you trudge up the stairs of this facility. *(It's even breath-taking going "down" the stairs.)*

My room was on the aforementioned *third floor*. Each trip back to my quarters required the aforementioned four or five-minute rest at the top of the stairs before I could advance any further.

> *Leadville, Colorado – due to its somewhat isolated and inhospitable location – has changed little from the Old West days of Holliday.*

(I moved a chair over to a spot near the top of the stairs in which I would partake of my "recovery" after each labored trip.)

Though some mining continues in Leadville today, the town now derives most of its income from tourism. Long gone are the fast times and fast money generated by the one-time mineral wealth of the area in the 1880s. Leadville, however, is very much worthwhile as a tourism destination.

The Delaware was built in 1886, and it may or may not have been patronized by John Henry Holliday. He left Leadville in 1887, spending the final months of his life in Glenwood Springs prior to his death there in November of that year. If he did not visit the Delaware, however, it would be one of the few buildings in town which escaped his attentions, for he was surprisingly active in the community during his residence there, moving from saloon to saloon to ply his trade.

The accommodations at the Delaware are acceptable, if somewhat spartan. This is assuming one doesn't mind somewhat smallish rooms, and a shower which runs icy cold and scalding hot intermittently as one bathes. I'm not too picky, but my sweet wife was considerably less forgiving.

At the time we were there, a complimentary breakfast was served for patrons of the hotel each morning, and I can honestly say it was a very good meal each day. This wasn't just a coffee and Danish breakfast. It was a full ride – oatmeal, eggs, toast, sausage, bacon – the works. It was delicious.

Doc's Old Hotel

During my first day in Leadville, I walked down Main Street (Harrison Ave.) to 316 Harrison to the old hotel/saloon (originally Mannie Hyman's Saloon) in which Doc had lived and worked from 1882 to 1887. This saloon was also the site of Holliday's last gunfight in which he shot (and almost killed) Billy Allen in 1884.

Though some historians have questioned their authenticity, a number of dental tools and at least one pistol supposedly once owned by Holliday were displayed upon the walls of this former saloon. I found myself seeking out the site of the former "cigar stand" where Holliday took refuge as he awaited Allen that day.

Doc's room in this historic building was upstairs on the northwest corner. It is seven-by-fourteen feet in size and was open to the public on occasion for viewing when I was there, although the owner wanted to charge me just for a visit to peek into the room. I declined.

In the 1880s, Mannie Hyman rented nine rooms in this building to various individuals. Holliday's room included a view through the front window of the snow-covered peaks of the Rocky Mountains.

Although Doc was a faro dealer in Hyman's, he also regularly gambled himself in John G. Morgan's Board of Trade Saloon across the street, as well as in a number of other saloons and gambling establishments in town. The Board of Trade building, which also still stands, was called the Silver Dollar Saloon during my visit. Its owners – as it turned out – became an important source of bail money after Holliday's arrest for the Billy Allen shooting.

The Last Gunfight

In his day, John Henry Holliday developed a strong friendship with the Board of Trade's owners – John Morgan and Col. Samuel Houston – and it later proved to be a valuable association. When he was arrested for shooting Billy Allen, Holliday was destitute, and so sick he could no longer support himself as a gambler. As a result, he could not raise bail, and undoubtedly would have been forced to endure a long very cold incarceration in jail prior to his trial had not Morgan and Houston stepped forward.

Together, the two merchants quickly posted the $5,000 bail money – a considerable sum in the 1880s – and Holliday was released to return to his sick-bed until the day of his trial. He subsequently was justifiably acquitted of the charges against him.

As I strolled about the main room of the old Hyman saloon, imagining the circumstances of the gunfight, the owner pointed out many details concerning the incident, showing me the spot at which Holliday had stood as he fired, and the spot at which Allen had fallen after being wounded.

Billy Allen was an old enemy of Holliday's, dating back to the Tombstone days in 1881. In an amazing stroke of bad luck, the weakened Holliday had the misfortune to be in Leadville at the same time as did Allen, who was a friend of the Clantons, a family of outlaws who had opposed the Earps and Holliday during their days in Arizona.

Allen had also testified against Holliday at the Inquest following the shooting at the O.K. Corral, and a number of individuals – including Doc himself – believed Allen had fired several shots at them during the Tombstone fracas. For was a confrontation which was almost inevitable.

Despite the fact that Holliday was almost defenseless by this time *(He had ceased carrying a handgun, since he could not afford the fine if he were caught carrying a concealed weapon.)*, he seemed to find an inner resolve which enabled him to deal with the situation.

As an indication of just how desperate Doc had become by this point, he had fallen into a trap set by the trouble-maker Allen, borrowing $5.00 from him for a gambling stake. When he was unable to repay the loan at the appointed hour, Allen began publicly bullying and humiliating him.

Doc eventually received word that his tormentor was coming to pay him a final visit, and that if he did not come forth with the overdue $5.00, a physical beating at the very least would be forthcoming. In the end, however, it was Allen who ended up writhing upon the floor, with Doc escaping uninjured. It was interesting to visit the building where that drama had finally played out.

Leadville was very cold – in the 30s – the day I visited in the month of September. There was snow on the ground and more snow falling. I can only assume it was much the same during Holliday's stay, and despite the liveliness of the saloons and gambling opportunities at the time, the town must have been a lonely place for him in the 1880s.

Other Sites In Leadville

I next went up the hill to the *Leadville, Colorado & Southern (LC&S)* railroad depot three blocks northeast of the main street. This depot was built in 1893 to service the *Denver, South Park & Pacific (DSP&P)* and *Colorado & Southern (C&S)* railroads. Since Holliday departed Leadville in 1887, he never

BOARD OF TRADE SALOON - Opened originally as the Board of Trade saloon in 1879, the facility at 313 Harrison Avenue was known more recently as the "Silver Dollar Saloon," a novelty and collectibles shop. From 1882 to 1886 however, when it was actually a saloon and gambling establishment, it was regularly patronized by Holliday during his off hours when he wasn't working across the street in Hyman's Saloon. The owners of the Board of Trade were the individuals who bailed Doc out of jail following the Billy Allen shooting in Leadville. (Photo by Olin Jackson)

this and other reasons, Allen and Holliday were anything but friends.

By the time Doc and Allen met again in Leadville, Holliday was much weaker and sicker, and Allen no doubt saw an opportunity to gain a reputation for himself as the individual who finally got the drop on the famed gunman. It used the *DSP&P* or the *C&S* railroads or the associated depot, but this facility was patronized by a number of other notables.

Other railroad lines, however, had preceded these into Leadville, and almost certainly were patronized by Holliday in his numerous travels to and from the town. The *Denver & Rio Grande* had arrived in 1880, and the *Colorado Midland* arrived in 1887. Though he almost certainly used these rail lines as his diminishing funds allowed, Doc, more often than not, traveled within the freezing confines of a jarring stagecoach, since it was less expensive.

When I was there, the *LC&S* railroad offered an awe-inspiring excursion ride on the old rail line. The trip lasts two and one-half hours and takes passengers high into the Rockies to the continental divide. Although the cost seemed somewhat pricey to me at the time ($24 for adults; $12.50 for children), I am told this ride is well-worth the money.

There were many other buildings and interesting spots to visit in this town from yesteryear. After several days, in this vicinity, however, I was ready to move on. I was restless just as I suspect Holliday eventually became, though he spent much more time here than did I.

Gunning For Gunnison

Our next destination was Gunnison, Colorado. We arose at 7:15 a.m. the next morning and enjoyed our last breakfast in the famed Delaware. After loading up our rented Dodge Durango, we headed south on U.S. 24 to U.S. 285 and thence to U.S. 50. This was an amazingly beautiful drive, and should not be missed if ever one has the opportunity to enjoy it. Huge towering snow-capped peaks and very striking rock formations all along this route make it a fascinatingly scenic route.

We finally reached Monarch Pass high in the mountains, and I thought at first that we were going to have to use snow-chains to make it through the pass. Fortunately there had not been an accumulation of ice, and so the chains were not necessary. During winter months, however, snow chains very definitely would be required in the higher elevations such as this – and that's assuming the route would even be open, as it often is not in winter.

We drove through deep snow for a number of miles *(Remember, this was in September when the temperatures were in the 80s and 90s in Georgia.)* before eventually dropping below the snow line again on the other side of the pass.

We finally reached Gunnison after a full day's ride. I could see why this town was chosen by Wyatt and Warren Earp as a spot to spend the summer of 1882. They had just finished their "Vendetta Ride" in Arizona, and were on the run from what at the time were corrupt Arizona authorities.

The remote and isolated location of Gunnison offered just the peace and solitude the Earps and Doc no doubt were seeking at that time. This tiny mountain community is located in a broad, somewhat fertile valley at the top of the Colorado Rockies. It would have been very difficult to reach – especially by someone on horseback in the 1880s.

According to records, the Earps camped outside town for the entire summer, but Doc, preferring an easier life in the hotels of Denver, only remained for a week or so. Gunnison becomes brutally cold in the winter (with temperatures reportedly at minus 20 degrees Fahrenheit), so camping in any season other than summer simply is not feasible.

Though the town of Leadville had seemed somewhat limited in scope, the town of Gunnison was even smaller, but there seemed to be a bit more "new" and promising modern development here. Doc, however, felt Gunnison was simply too primitive for his tastes, and moved on to Denver for a few months before eventually traveling to Leadville. Wyatt and Warren eventually drifted back southwestward to California and Warren – amazingly – went back to Arizona a year or two later to work on a cattle farm only a short distance from Tombstone where the Earp family had suffered so much harm.

Hooray For Ouray

Judy and I continued our drive along beautiful Blue Mesa Lake (Colorado's largest) for many miles. We witnessed still more amazing stretches of breath-taking scenery. This drive from Leadville to Ouray and on to Telluride has to be one of the most beautiful in America.

We turned onto U.S. Highway 550 and after additional miles, finally reached our next destination – historic Ouray, Colorado. This town also was a gold-mining community after the precious yellow metal was discovered there in 1875.

It is not known by this writer if Holliday traveled to this vicinity during his wanderings to various gambling opportunities in Colorado, but the Earps, in fact, did spend time here. Though Holliday crisscrossed this vicinity in the 1880s, and therefore could easily have passed time as well in Ouray, it would have been an obscure visit at best, since no mention of it has been found in historic records. That absence of a record of his visit to this town, however, means nothing, since much of Doc's wanderings were

done with no mention or record of his visits whatsoever, and often under an assumed name.

Ouray was on the route the Earps would have taken from Gunnison back to California. We followed what appeared to be portions of an old trace on our route to this mountainous town, and on several occasions I in fact did see historic markers along the way identifying it as the old stagecoach trail, so it almost certainly was the route followed by the Earps.

The magnificent surroundings of Ouray – the San Juan Mountains – are awe-inspiring to say the least, rising to 14,000 feet. A photograph or verbal description simply does not do this area justice. These peaks form an unbelievable back-drop for the elegant Victorian homes and old West commercial buildings of this town, many of which were built between 1880 and 1900.

The population of Ouray is only 800 permanent residents year-round, and that's one of the things I liked best about this locale. It not only is an unbelievably scenic area, but a very peaceful one as well. It is located at 7,770 feet so it's high enough that you know you're in the Colorado Rockies, but low enough to have pleasing weather year-round.

A typical summer day in Ouray is sunny, with temperatures in the 70s and sometimes even in the 80s. Evening temperatures range in the 50s. A typical winter averages 140 inches of snowfall and the days are sunny and bright with highs averaging in the 40s and lows in the high teens. It gets plenty cold enough to provide a favorable environment for lots of snow, but it's not unbearably cold – just the way I like it. Although it is not necessary, it is strongly advisable to drive only a four-wheel drive vehicle with snow tires or chains during the winter.

SCENIC OURAY – Located high in the Colorado Rockies, this quaint mountain town was yet another site of mining after gold was discovered here in 1875. Many renowned figures from the Old West have been documented as having passed through this tiny town. Wyatt and Warren Earp are known to have spent time here, as also undoubtedly did John Henry Holliday, although his presence has not been documented. The scenic quality of this site also drew Hollywood movie-makers in 1968, for the filming of scenes from the *Academy Award*-winning motion picture, ***True Grit***, starring John Wayne, Glen Campbell, Robert Duvall, and Kim Darby. (Photo by Olin Jackson)

PIONEER TRACE – Located on an ages-old travel route between what today are Arizona and Colorado, numerous noted figures from the Old West passed through Ouray, Colorado. A 1800s-era stagecoach trail along this route is identified today by historic markers. (Photo by Olin Jackson)

Our accommodations in Ouray were at the St. Elmo Hotel. This marvelous old inn near the downtown area was built in 1898, and – just as many other historic buildings in this town – still exists almost as it did when built over 100 years ago. I was not able to learn if one of the aged commercial buildings on the old main street of this town once served as a hotel in which a wandering John Henry Holliday might have passed time. I did, however discover that another historic figure from the old West spent time here.

True Grit

The next morning, we emerged for a visit to the old downtown area of Ouray. It was because of the scenic beauty and Old West atmosphere here that selected spots in Ouray and the adjacent community of Ridgway were used in the filming of the 1969 major motion picture, *True Grit*. Starring John Wayne, Kim Darby, Glen Campbell and Robert Duvall, this award-winning movie is still one of the most popular Westerns ever filmed, earning the "Duke" an *Academy Award* for his performance.

Interestingly, the old courthouse in the middle of Ouray was the site at which the *True Grit* courthouse scenes with Wayne were filmed. As we were leaving this town several days later, I was able to stop at Ridgway a few miles away to see where Wayne had performed in other scenes from the movie filmed in that town. Interestingly, a young Marion Morrison – prior to his identity as John Wayne – both knew and occasionally conversed with an aging Wyatt Earp in the late 1920s in Hollywood when Earp was acting as an advisor to the new-fangled movie productions attempting to portray the Old West.

I later traveled to other scenic destinations in Colorado, New Mexico and Texas on this same trip. The only other town I visited, however which was also visited by Holliday was Dallas, Texas, ironically where Doc's travels in the old West had begun so many years ago. Today, just as in Denver, Holliday's tracks in fast-moving Dallas have also been erased forever by modern development.

Prior to Dallas, I made additional stops at historic Telluride, Colorado. While I was there, I was able to visit the old San Miguel Valley Bank building (still extant on Main Street in Telluride) which was robbed by Butch Cassidy and three accomplices in 1889, two years after Doc's death. And as a juxtaposition of time eras, I couldn't help but smile at the fact that just a few hundred yards away, the famous (and now no longer existent) *Allman Brothers Band* was performing one of their last concerts.

Following my departure from Telluride, I drove down State Highway 145 which is an ancient travel route through the Rockies, originally cut by migratory animals in prehistory. This trail subsequently fell into use by Native Americans and still later by white settlers as a stage coach route. According to records, Cassidy traversed this route many times as he rustled horses to sell in Telluride. He also followed it as he fled Telluride after robbing the bank there in 1889.

It is not known by this writer if Doc Holliday traversed this vicinity in southwestern Colorado, but Wyatt and Warren Earp almost certainly did. If you're looking for an interesting vacation in some very historic Old West towns, visit the places described above. You'll be glad you did, and along the way, you'll gain an appreciation for the rugged life endured by those hardy travelers of yesteryear – particularly John Henry Holliday.

The Last Days of John Henry Holliday

Though the actual circumstances of John Henry Holliday's last days on this earth have been debated for decades, a credible recently-discovered newspaper article possibly describes the actual events, and debunks some previously-held notions.

Some writers and researchers have maintained that John Henry Holliday spent his last days alone in the Hotel Glenwood, slowly wasting away until death finally took him. Other researchers, supported by at least one recently-discovered document, however, maintain an entirely different set of circumstances existed. Until recent times, no detailed first-hand account of Doc's last days was known to exist, but an 1889 issue of the *Sulphur Headlight* newspaper may have changed all that.

According to Karen Holliday Tanner, Doc summoned his long-time consort – Katherine "Big Nose Kate" Harony – when he realized his last days were upon him, and she subsequently traveled to his bedside, caring for him until he died. However, very little if any corroborating evidence of this or many of the other details of Holliday's last hours were known to exist – that is until the February 14, 1899 issue of the *Sulphur Headlight* of Sulphur, Oklahoma, came to light.

The information was detailed by an individual named Origen C. "Harelip Charlie" Smith, a bonafide ally of the Earps and Holliday during the volatile days in Tombstone, Arizona Territory, in 1880-1882. Smith was a business associate of Bob Winders in Tombstone, and had allied himself with the Earps in support of law and order in the frontier town. His days in that town are well-documented, and are a matter of public record today. He was respected as knowledgeable and trustworthy by associates in Tombstone, so there is little reason to doubt his claims.

By coincidence, Smith found himself traveling in the same stagecoach as Holliday to Glenwood Springs, Colorado, in 1887, and even living in the same hotel there as Doc. According to the *Headlight* article, Smith was present during Holliday's dying days and was intimately familiar with the individuals present and the events surrounding the last hours of the celebrated Georgian.

Later, after moving back to Tombstone, Arizona, Smith, realizing the importance of the body of knowledge he carried with him regarding his Tombstone days and the years thereafter, began writing down his memoirs for posterity. He reportedly sought out an old friend – Lundsford Bryant Shockley – to collaborate with him on the memoirs. Though there is no specific reason to doubt Smith's veracity or the accuracy of his memory in describing Holliday's last hours, it of course is not impossible that portions of his recollections were imprecise.

In 1899, Shockley reportedly shared the portion of Smith's memoirs involving Doc Holliday's last days in Glenwood Springs with the publisher of the **Sulphur** (Oklahoma) **Headlight**. Why he chose to share Smith's work with this particular newspaper at this particular point in time is unknown today. He was living in the Indian Territory near Sulphur, Oklahoma, at the time, which provides a measure of explanation for his use of that town's newspaper. Whatever the circumstances, on February 14 of that year, the **Headlight** published the very interesting details of Doc's last days as drawn from Shockley's revelation of Smith's memoirs.

The article from the **Headlight** is re-published here in its entirety, exactly as written by Smith, with the exception of quotation marks and paragraph delineations for ease of reading. The article is very detailed, and includes considerable information which would have been exceedingly difficult to fabricate had not the writer actually been present as a witness at Holliday's death. The initial portion of the article was written from the editor's perspective, with the remainder from Smith's perspective. It reads as follows:

"The story comes to the **Headlight** *from colleague Lundsford Shockley, resident of the Chickasaw Nations, Ardmore, Indian Territory. It is known that Mr. Shockley came to town by wagon early in the evening and boarded at the Hotel Sulphur Springs in preparation to meet the* **Headlight** *staff.*

"It is apparent that connections to Mr. [Origen Charles] Smith came from Shockley's days with John Roberts of the [John] Slaughter crew, driving those vast

Texas herds up to the San Pedro Valley. Shockley comments: 'We were encamped up in the Sierra Vistas in '81. On the first time out, many of the boys wanted to go to Tombstone and experience the town's pleasures. Tombstone was a mining camp built from the dust much like the old pueblo, Tucson, which offered a cowboy anything imaginable.'

"According to Charlie Smith, it was also a community built on politics; 'a common cause of much of the troubles there.'

"When upon reading the Harelip Smith papers, I might comment that the significance surrounds the death of John H. Holliday, known as Doc, on November 8, 1887, where Smith occupied a room across the hallway from him in the Hotel Glenwood, some twelve years ago. It is important to note that Origen Smith's recollections serve as a standard account of the dentist's last days in Glenwood Springs who wrote on his Sol Israel stationary on October 8, 1887, that Holliday was confined to his bed by the local physician who had told his [Doc's] mistress: 'I have done all that can be done. It is in John's hands now. And God's.'

"Origen Smith gives an account of Doc Holliday's arrival to the mountain resort on May 24, 1887 [as follows]:

"'The Concorde coach had slammed into the rocks along the narrow gauge of mountain road near Carbondale, which damaged the wheel at the rear of the coach which suddenly ended their journey until a mechanic could be brought in from several miles distant. The narrow gauge out of Leadville was hard on Holliday and its three passengers, but it was the best means of travel for the day.

"'The three passengers on the stage knew who Doc Holliday was, but I doubt they had heard of Origen Smith when I arrived on the Leadville laundry train with a group of miners who flooded Leadville

when *Hoarse Tabot* [Horace "Haw" Tabor] *discovered the "Matchbox"* [Matchless] *mine. We were packed in that coach like a can of sardines, fighting to get out.*

"'I had boarded the coach heeled but concealed it inside my coat just as Doc had done that day when all hell broke loose down at Montgomery's* [the O.K. Corral]. *In Tombstone, I had served as vigilance messenger for Colonel Wm. Herring, a prominent Tombstone attorney who's* [sic] *office located at 534 Freemont, served as a meeting place for many of Wyatt Earp's backers. In 1882, I had been a messenger for Wyatt, joining his federal posse after the death of his brother by cowards.*

"'Experience had taught me that a man like Holliday – who told me once that I should join the game – did not fear death. It was the living that he feared most. The fear of not going out game. Many times I had seen Doc cry tears from the agony the dreadful disease scourged him when the whiskey failed to do its work.*

"'The trip from Leadville* [to Glenwood Springs] *was hard on Doc. The jolting from the narrow gauge would cause him to cough up pieces of lung and blood. It was about two o'clock when the stage reached the Hotel Glenwood. Kate said it was May 24th.*

"'Doc was coughing from almost each breath and upon arrival, had to use his cane to support his weight. He was very frail in body when I saw him, and his hair was a silver gray. His face showed the lines of age and he looked sick in the eyes. His appearance resembled that of an older man, since pulling out of Hooker's Ranch* [outside Tombstone, AT,

where the Vendetta riders had been temporarily protected in 1882].

"'One might argue that Doc was content in his actions and that his daily consumption of whiskey came to be his only escape from his suffering. I was rightly taken with the general surroundings of Glenwood Springs upon reaching Eighth Avenue, holding my duffle and looking for the hotel.*

"Kate had told me Doc was boarding. All I wanted was to register and find a bathhouse. I had run into Kate in the lobby who had sent this young bellhop, whom Doc had nicknamed Kenny* [Art Kendrick], *on an errand.*

"'The welcome feeling I experienced far exceeded that of Tombstone I soon discovered. The district was full of excitement when the train pulled into the station house. I recall most of all how many people were about on the streets.*

"'There was a definite resemblance to Denver; the big blue sky and the "Rockies" that seem to surround the town, which I would soon see was a perfect view from Doc's hotel window.*

"'The Denver and Rio Grande* [which was completed into Glenwood Springs in 1887] *was due to arrive the following day* [October 5], *and the town was full of anticipation of the arrival of the new iron horse. Banners swung across streets, and merchant signs from store front windows. Great expectations filled the streets.*

"'I refrained from the moment and walked in the lobby of the Hotel Glenwood. The lobby was furnished with fine Victorian trimmings and elaborate knotted-Persian carpets, and reminded me of the Cosmopolitan

> *I had seen Doc cry tears from the agony the dreadful disease scourged him when the whiskey failed to do its work.*

This tombstone – though now replaced – existed for well over half a century in Linwood Cemetery outside Glenwood Springs, Colorado. It was erected after the tourism value of Doc Holliday's name had been realized by the residents of the town. Though his actual burial site has been a matter of complete conjecture almost from the day he was interred in 1887, the tombstone pictured here supposedly identified Holliday's grave at Linwood. Ironically, not only did it not identify the specific burial plot of the famed gunman, the engraving in the headstone contained numerous errors of fact, including the famous Georgian's birth site, birthday, and the medical school he attended. A replacement headstone erected in more recent years in Linwood, though correcting the errors of fact, nevertheless still does not identify the specific site of his grave, which some have even speculated now actually exists in Griffin, Georgia.

and Grand hotels in Tombstone, and the White Club House Room in Denver.

"'There was this need to put down words on paper since leaving Hooker's Ranch in '82, but it was Kate's enduring patience and devotion to Doc that gave me my inspiration to [finally] tell the story.

"'There was a sense of fatalism in Kate's voice, yet talk of the springs which had brought Doc to Glenwood was the last hope the West had to offer a lunger like Doc. I suppose if there was a chance for Doc's health to improve, he would take up its resources in Glenwood Springs.

"'Writing this down is not to judge him for past actions, but to understand him. Doc's memory seemed to be unaffected at times, although he lost much of his lungs over the years out West since leaving his beloved Georgia. I know the whiskey came to be his only escape from the pain that came with the consumption, and his desperate longing for home.

"'There is no doubt that the short time Doc lived inside the Hotel Glenwood, [it] became his sanctuary. What transpired within the walls will leave a lasting impression. One that is etched in my memory.

"Coming to Glenwood Springs with the miners in October, I found Doc delirious and dying. He had fallen to a pneumonia the local doctor said, and had not spoken a word in weeks. Kate was already there taken (sic) care of him when I arrived. She said Doc had sent word to her in Globe from Leadville and told her he was leaving after a bit of excitement with Will Allen, and was taking a stage to

HOTEL DENVER – The Leadville Bar in the Hotel Denver in Glenwood Springs no doubt experienced a crisis of identity at least occasionally. It was photographed circa 1890s, and quite possibly was visited by Holliday prior to his demise in Glenwood Springs. (Courtesy of Frontier Historical Society)

Glenwood Springs, in Garfield County to see if the sulfur springs would ease his consumption.

"Kate's devotion to Doc was not surprising, for she remained by his side till the end. Doc had tolerated my presence in Tombstone, though suggested I join the game after Morg's death, since Morg and I had a fondness to billiards at Robert Hatch's. Doc was still a young man though he began to deteriorate in Denver and became more advanced as his struggle for pain was no longer at his control. Doc was at the point of never leaving his bed again.

"'I imagine Kate felt helpless not being able to ease his pain. Shortly after Doc arrived, he tryed [sic] dealing faro but no longer could keep up the long hours he was used to in Tombstone, for he tired easily. Walking from gambling house to gambling house became an exhausting event, and the treatments at the springs [never] seemed to have any effect.

"'Kate was their means for support, for Doc could not work. I would help to bring in money by doing odd jobs around town, and doing mechanic work for a blacksmith shop.

"'Since October, Doc hardly spoke and hardly sat up twice. Kate never wanted to be far from Doc. I consoled her and saw to it no harm came to Doc from the traffic coming and going inside the hotel. Doc had made many enemies in his life and perhaps [because of] the troubles Doc faced in Arizona and Colorado, she still sensed danger to him.

"A light snow had fallen early in the morning and Kate had to shut the window in Doc's room. His breathing had become shallow overnight and the color in his face had turned pale. It is important to know the last day as I was in the hotel room with Doc and Kate as he clinged [sic] to life.

"An era was ending Kate thought. I don't write about an era changing, but a man's life who was shaped around it. For Kate the day began to fall apart when I was told that she sent for the doctor and that I should return to Doc's room. It seemed strange for anyone besides Doc or Kate to summon me at once. I went, expecting the end had come.

"In the lobby I had a strange feeling. Instead of the heavy traffic, there was this stillness in the hotel lobby as I hurried up to Doc's room. Then the bellhop told me that Doc was sitting up. I felt relief for Kate. For a moment I thought Doc had cheated death one last time.

"Doc had been found that morning sitting up by the maid who had awoke [sic] Kate who had slept in Doc's chair that he liked sitting by the window in. The doctor was there when I got there. He was saying something to Kate, but his words didn't make her feel better.

"For the first time in weeks, the details and the sound of Dr. B.'s [possibly Dr. Baldwin] voice was [sic] clear. She knew the end was upon him. Knowing Doc, I figured he might pull out another winning hand. It was not meant to be. This would be his last game.

"I did not know the complete story

His breathing had become shallow overnight and the color in his face had turned pale.

from the doctor who had been making house calls to Doc's room the past few weeks. Though I never doubted his opinion. In the final hour I knew one thing. Doc was about to cash in his chips.

"There were several Glenwood residents in the room, Sarah Copper [Sarah Field Cooper] and Walter Devereaux, whom [sic] [had] shared a seat with Doc on the Concorde stage.

"The doctor who had been sent for by Kenny stood over Doc pouring him a tumbler of whiskey, jotting down medical quotes [notes] in his notebook. During the final moments, when the end was approaching, Doc turned his head toward Kate and smiled. He turned up the tumbler with great fashion as he always had done in the past.

"As the light began to fade from his eyes, he took his last breath, and I heard him say, "This is funny." Then his eyes stood still, and his body relaxed. Doc was lying on his bed, dead. I remember Kate saying in a distraught voice, "The end of Holliday." The room seemed as lifeless as he was.

"He had opened his eyes once or twice that morning, but his gaze was clouded. When I saw him open his eyes at Kate, she leaned over him straining to hear something or read something from his eyes. Kate was trying to tell him something, though I doubt he heard her. The Colt, which he employed laid idle in the bureau, retired for all times. "Doc is at peace, Charlie. The worms won't get Doc today."

"It is unthinkable, but during his time of dying, I realized the loss that Kate was feeling. In the beginning when I first met him in Tombstone, he had been a sporting man, usually staying among Wyatt's crowd, yet everyone who knew him was certain of his loyalty to friends.

"'Doc didn't have many friends, and he showed honor to the ones he did have. Those in the room were showing their respect for Doc. During the moment when he at last found peace, and the pain had left him, I knew he had found what he longed for. Doc had died a slow, lingering death.

"'It would surprise him to have escaped death so many times, to have died in a room in Glenwood Springs. At the end when Doc was gone, the doctor noted the time of death. "Nine fifty-five, November 8, 1887."

"'Preparations were made for a quick funeral, which would take place in a place called Linwood, a short distance by hack at two o'clock the same day. It would be a quiet procession, with the Reverend Rudolph officiating. His coffin would be elaborate with silver trimmings, donated by Glenwood's social class and friends he had made.

"'By 11 o'clock, the undertakers came to remove Doc's body from the hotel. It was the first time I had seen the physical scars the consumption had left on his body. The body was taken away. A black hearse rolled to a stop near the front entrance, and everybody came outside. Those who were standing on the boardwalk and those in the street tipped their hats to Kate as the hearse drove away.

"'Kate left Glenwood Springs after Doc's possessions were in order to be sent back to relatives in Georgia. It was a sad parting. I left November 10th, the day after Kate. Will stop by Leadville to see Bob I think.'"

This article confirms that Kate Harony did in fact come to Doc's aid during his last days

It is interesting to note from the above article that several items which have been questioned over the years as to their authenticity can now quite possibly be certified as being accurate as a result of this article.

First of all, this article confirms that Kate Harony did in fact come to Doc's aid during his last days, staying with him and caring for him until the end. The article also gives a specific date (May 24, 1887) for Doc's arrival in Glenwood Springs. Prior to this article, it was known only that he had arrived in the spring of 1887.

Also confirmed by the article is the fact that Art Kendrick ("Kenny") – who long claimed he was the bellhop in the Hotel Glenwood during Doc's last days and ran many errands for him – was also actually telling the truth about those experiences.

Finally, one of the most enduring legends of the Old West is also put to bed with this article, since it seems to confirm – despite many claims to the contrary – that Doc did indeed quite possibly utter the famous words *"This is funny"* in a final moment of lucidness shortly before his death, acknowledging the humor in the fact that he was dying with his boots off.

Though Origen C. "Harelip Charley" Smith seems to be attempting to a great degree to weave in his own history with that of John Henry Holliday and the Earp faction with his memoirs, he does, nevertheless, provide and corroborate a number of previously-unknown valuable details regarding the history and legend of John Henry Holliday.

Buried in Colorado or Georgia?

Where Lie The Bones Of John Henry Holliday?

He is one of the most celebrated figures of the old West, but today,
"Doc" Holliday's final resting place is completely unknown. . . . or is it?

Many of the locations of the last remains of popular figures from the old West are known quite well today. Interestingly, however, the specific location of the last remains of one of the most famous figures in the old West is a total mystery today.

But strangely, that actually isn't that unusual, particularly for old West gunmen. They often were buried where they fell – and fairly quickly before putrefaction could set in. Their graves also invariably were very poorly marked for posterity – more often than not without permanent stone markers.

For instance, no one today knows the "exact" gravesite of William H. Bonney, alias "Billy the Kid" – though his is at least known generally. Not so, however for Butch Cassidy, nor "the Sundance Kid," nor "Curly Bill" Brocius, nor "Buckskin" Frank Leslie, nor "Turkey Creek" Jack Johnson, nor Warren Earp, and on and on, all of whose graves are a total mystery today. Strange? You be the judge.

Most of these men were intentionally mysterious in life, often identifying themselves by aliases, and secretively withholding almost all actual details about themselves and their familial

background for their entire lives. So what's so unusual about that circumstance carrying over into death? John Henry Holliday himself occasionally used an alias when he was "on the run." He also played the facts of his life "very close to the vest" while he was alive, though the mystery about his actual gravesite is just a bit different.

John Henry Holliday's parents – Henry Burroughs Holliday and Alice Jane McKey – were from South Carolina, before moving to Georgia. They provided a good education for their son, but his primary interest was the great outdoors. Nothing interested young John Henry more than hunting, fishing and horseback riding in what then was still a rolling wilderness in the Georgia back-country. In time, he also became intensely interested in the use of firearms as did many young men of his day. Some of these men became very adept in the use of weapons; some others not so much.

In 1861, Henry Burroughs Holliday accepted a presidential appointment from Jefferson Davis to serve as quartermaster in the 27th Georgia Infantry, Confederate States of America. After the Battle of Manassas, Henry

Burroughs was promoted to the rank of major and fought in the Peninsula Campaign as well as in the deadly Battle of Malvern Hill.

In 1862, a short time after fighting at Malvern Hill, Major Holliday was forced by ill health – watery dysentery – to leave the army and return to his family in Griffin. He, no doubt, thought death for him was eminent at that time, as ultimately became the case for most individuals suffering from this malady. He, however, somehow managed to survive. Approximately 26 years later, he would suffer through the mortality of his famous son, John Henry.

Creation Of A Myth

During his lifetime, John Henry was credited with the deaths of a number of men who were actually shot by other individuals.[1] The newspapers of that day – in the absence of factual information – often chose to simply fabricate the identity of those responsible for deaths, and once he had gained a bit of notoriety, John Henry Holliday suffered from this misidentification quite a bit. It just made for better reading, and, subsequently, better sales of the publications in which these defamatory statements were made.

With its usual artistic license, Hollywood also created a false image and persona for John Henry Holliday. In most instances, it portrayed him as a bloodthirsty and cold-blooded killer.

In reality, of the handful of shootings in which Holliday was actually involved, they occurred because much larger and stronger men – who, due to John Henry's much weaker and therefore vulnerable physical condition – tried to increase their own stature at his expense by attempting to either severely injure him, or kill him outright. These attackers, however, almost always misjudged their opponent when his name was Holliday.

Rather than resulting in John Henry's submission or serious injury or death, these attacks invariably ended in either a gun or a knife fight with Holliday virtually always gaining the upper hand. John Henry was weak and small in stature physically. There was no doubt about that. He, however, had been blessed with strong arms and hands, lightning-quick reflexes, and deadly accuracy with firearms, and he used all of his advantages – physical and mental – when attacked. And those who attacked him almost always regretted it too – if they lived to rue the day.

Doc Holliday's life contradicts the myth of the man. He was not a ruthless individual, nor was he "blood-thirsty" in nature, nor necessarily evil. *"When any of you fellows have been hunted from one end of the country to the other, as I have been, you'll understand what a bad man's reputation is built on,"* John Henry is reported to have once quipped.

Holliday pursued life under the only circumstances available to him. He sought to remain alive as long as his body would allow him, and along the way, unfortunately, his reputation from incidents in which he was forced to defend himself became twisted and tainted, and caused violence to follow him just as do fleas a dog. This myth of his preponderance or desire for violence, however, is just one of many which followed him into the grave.

Lost Burial Site

Inaccurate information seemed to plague Doc in death just as it had in real life. His obituary was printed in a variety of newspapers, but very few if any of them printed factual information about him or his death.

The local newspaper in Glenwood Springs, Colorado (where he died),

81

stated that Doc was buried *"in Linwood Cemetery,"* Glenwood Springs, Colorado, at 4:00 p.m., November 8, 1887. However, the steep trail that led to the cemetery (which exists on a hilltop mesa) reportedly was impassable due to snow and ice on the day Holliday's mortal remains were to be interred.

According to records, Doc was therefore actually buried in a temporary grave someplace near the foot of the hill. When spring and warmer weather returned, even if a burial detail had been organized to dig up his body to re-bury it in the cemetery-proper, no such re-burial ever occurred. As the years passed, the grave of John Henry Holliday was simply forgotten, and eventually, no one knew the site of his grave at all – just as they still do not today. Despite this fact, the signage in Linwood and the media accounts of his death and burial have consistently maintained that he is buried *"in Linwood Cemetery."*

The same Glenwood Springs newspaper which misstated the site of his burial also stated that many friends attended Holliday's funeral, but since he reportedly was buried the same day he died, this too is doubtful.[2] Also, adding insult to injury, both a monument and Holliday's headstone in Linwood Cemetery contained numerous mistakes for many years. It was almost as if his detractors were attempting to harass him even in death.

Tombstone, Arizona historian Ben Traywick seemed to state it best: *"It is difficult to see how so many mistakes could be made on a headstone without trying,"* he wrote.[3]

Despite the fact that a monument in Linwood Cemetery continues to proclaim that Holliday is buried *"somewhere in this cemetery,"* some historians today are convinced he was not.

One account maintains that following the spring thaw in 1888, a relative of Holliday's traveled to Glenwood Springs, retrieved the famous Georgian's body, and returned with it to that state where it was re-interred in Oak Hill Cemetery in Griffin, his boyhood home. Bill Dunn, a distant relative of Holliday's who headed up the *Doc Holliday Society* in Griffin, extensively researched the Holliday family for a number of years, and has an opinion of his own on this issue.

"There is no doubt in my mind why the people in Glenwood Springs don't know exactly where Doc is buried," Dunn said in an interview in 1999. "[It's because] he isn't there. *Doc is buried right here in his hometown of Griffin. He was originally buried near Linwood Cemetery, but he is not there now. You just don't lose the grave of a man who held his celebrity status."*

Buried In Georgia?

Some researchers believe that Doc's father, Major Henry B. Holliday (or his emissary) traveled to Glenwood Springs and claimed his son's remains. In retrospect, this is a definite possibility, since transportation of the coffin and remains could easily have been accomplished via the Denver & Rio Grande Western (D&RGW) Railroad which had been completed to Glenwood Springs in 1887 – the year Holliday died and prior to his death. And back in Griffin, Georgia, the train depot was within a mile of Oak Hill Cemetery.

Dunn says he believes that if it was not Major Holliday who retrieved his son's remains, he quite possibly sent his nephew, Robert Alexander Holliday, to perform the task. Doc's consort out West – Mary Katherine Harony – recalled in a later interview that one of Doc's cousins visited him in Tombstone after the shootout at the O.K. Corral. Dunn says he believes this man was Robert.

Strangely coincidental – or maybe not – is the fact that the final resting place of Major Holliday himself is also unknown today. Considering the fact that Henry Burroughs Holliday was a wealthy landowner, a decorated veteran of three wars, and a four-time mayor of Valdosta, Georgia, it is highly unlikely that his final resting place would not have been both clearly marked and definitely known today – unless he intentionally made arrangements to be buried in a secret location for a particular reason.

Major Holliday outlived his son by several years. He died on February 22, 1893 in Valdosta. Despite many years of searches, the location of his grave has eluded researchers just as has that of his famous son.

Bill Dunn maintains that he has located a marked grave for every Holliday family member in Valdosta and Griffin – except for Major Holliday and his son, John Henry. Dunn says he now believes without a doubt he has found the unmarked graves of both in Griffin's Oak Hill Cemetery.

The Plot Thickens

The two graves which Dunn says belong to Henry Burroughs and John Henry Holliday are located in the Thomas family plot at Oak Hill. The families enjoyed a very close relationship, and Dunn says he believes the Thomas family may have agreed to an anonymous burial of the two men in their family plot to avoid vandalism of the graves.

"I believe they buried Doc in Oak Hill when he was brought back from Glenwood Springs, and Major Holliday was buried there when he died," Dunn remarks. "Why would a plot containing expensive marble markers of the Thomas family contain two concrete slab graves with no marking or identification whatsoever? Could it be that they wanted them to remain anonymous and their last remains protected from vandalism?"

Osgood Miller, an employee of *Clark Monument Company* for forty-six years, once made a statement which lends credence to Dunn's claim. He said he remembered the late Charlie McElroy – who was cemetery superintendent during the 1930s – telling him that Doc Holliday was buried in Oak Hill. Osgood said Charlie even pointed in the direction of the Thomas plot when he made the statement. Several years later, the late Griffin historian Laura Clark pointed out the same area as Doc's final resting place.

Wyatt Earp, who was probably the closest friend John Henry Holliday ever had, died in 1929. Ironically, after all the gunfights in which he was involved, Earp was never once wounded. He died in bed from what undoubtedly was prostate cancer (listed as "prostatitis" on his death certificate).

While he and Doc were both still alive, Earp was quoted as saying *"Doc Holliday is the nerviest, fastest, deadliest man with a six-gun I ever saw."* And in Denver, Colorado, when last the two met and he realized that his old friend was near death, Earp, with tears in his eyes, also told Holliday that *"You saved my life on two separate occasions. Isn't it strange that you must go first."*

One can only marvel today that the final resting place of such a celebrated figure of the old West is, for all intents and purposes, completely unknown, as is that of his father, Henry Burroughs Holliday.

Endnotes

1/ *John Henry by Ben T. Traywick*
2/ *Ibid*
3/ *Ibid*

The Acquaintances of Doc Holliday

What do we know today that can be confirmed as factual information regarding the "friendly" and "adversarial" acquaintances of John Henry Holliday? Well, according to Doc's first cousin, the "friends" comprise a short list, but then, she didn't seem to try very hard. Admittedly, however, the list of individuals who despised and wished ill of him certainly seems lengthier than that of those who loved or admired him.

For more than a century now, the gunfight behind the O.K. Corral in Arizona Territory in 1881 has carried the dubious distinction as "one of the most confusing 15 seconds in American history." Even more conflicting, however, are the various modern descriptions of the relationships John Henry Holliday had with his various acquaintances in the West.

Fanned by ceaseless rumors and the imaginations of the masses, as well as the countless erroneous articles and portrayals from the days of dime novels in the late 19th Century all the way up to the modern books and major motion pictures of the present-day, the confusing brushfire that supposedly represents the real Doc Holliday of Western lore continues to burn unabated.

Susan McKey Thomas is Holliday's first cousin once-removed. Perhaps it is appropriate that her educated, scrupulously studied opinions of Doc become, if not the last word, at least a part of the final sentence.

"Cousin Mattie" (Sister Mary Melanie)

It seems to go without saying, that any list of Doc's acquaintances with whom he had a positive or favorable relationship has to include cousin Mattie Holliday, daughter of Robert K. Holliday of Jonesboro, Georgia. In his early life, John Henry had played and enjoyed secrets with Mattie that were shared with no one else. This relationship supposedly grew into much more than just friendship. It goes without saying that Mattie quite possibly had a much stronger bond with him than anyone else.

When the relationship turned from friendship to whatever it later became is anyone's guess today. Whatever the circumstances, when John Henry left his Georgia home, though it was claimed that he departed for dryer climes for health reasons, some have speculated that the departure also involved some type of unfortunate incident which had occurred between him and cousin Mattie.

At approximately the same point as Doc's relocation to the West, Mattie had suddenly entered a Catholic convent, taking her vows and remaining in that capacity for the rest of her life. It is a matter of record that John Henry mourned the loss of his relationship with Mattie for the remainder of his life.

GRAND AVENUE – This main thoroughfare in Glenwood Springs was photographed on June 18, 1898, a little over 10 years after Holliday's death. The gambler from Georgia strode down this street more than a few times. Visible on the right side of the street in the distance is the Hotel Glenwood in which he died.

Despite this fact, he and Mattie continued to communicate by letter long after he had relocated – reportedly quite often. Very personal and engaging letters which no doubt revealed a side of John Henry unknown to the outside world.

When John Henry finally passed away due to the ravages of tuberculosis, Sister Mary Melanie reportedly burned the letters she had received from him, in order that they not fall into the hands of others and be misinterpreted after her death. For many years thereafter, as a result of the harsh and negative publicity which had grown up around John Henry's name before and after his death, Sister Mary stated openly that had she not burned the letters, the world would have known a much different John Henry Holliday than the one portrayed in the harsh and sensationalized Western mythology that had become so prominent and unattractive.

"Big Nose Kate"

Aside from the famous incident behind the O.K. Corral in Tombstone, Arizona Territory, in October of 1881, one of the few things about which most historians agree regarding Holliday was his intimate relationship with Mary Katherine Harony (Haroney) Cummings, a.k.a. "Big-Nose" Kate Elder, a prostitute who was known by at least seven different identities during her life. She appears to have been the gunfighter's only romantic interest of consequence after he left Georgia.

Though she passes no judgment on the Holliday-Harony/Cummings coupling, Ms. Thomas says with no reservation that no official marriage ever took place regarding the pair, in spite of the fact that many sources accept the marriage as fact and Harony/Cummings herself was vehement in her assertions that she was Doc's widow.

Ms. Thomas maintains a long list of evidence to back up her assertion to the contrary.

"There are so many reasons not to believe he was ever married to Katie Elder," Ms. Thomas explained in an interview in 2001. *"When she told the story, she said they were married in Valdosta, supposedly on a visit in 1880, and she gave a date. Well, the marriages of that period are available on record, and there is no record of any marriage between Doc and Katie."*

Thomas's argument is augmented by the fact that Doc Holliday almost certainly never returned to Georgia after traveling to the West. Thomas maintained that most of what Doc's immediate family even knew of the prodigal son after he traveled to the West was gleaned from the **Valdosta Daily Times** newspaper.

Then there also is the family **Bible**.

"I have an authentic copy of the records in the family Bible," Ms. Thomas continued. *"Now his father was a meticulous man, and in that Bible are entries of births, deaths – anything that pertained to the family. The major almost certainly would have entered the marriage – whether he approved of it or not – and he did not enter anything about such a marriage."*

Although Doc Holliday did not correspond with his Valdosta relatives, it is a matter of record that he did write regularly to Mattie (Sister Mary Melanie). There is a great probability that Sister Mary would have passed along the news of such a marriage, unless Doc specifically instructed her to the contrary, which of course is always possible.

According to Ms. Thomas, however, there is even more evidence of the absence of such a marriage. *"Katie told an interviewer about their relationship, and not only did she not know the names of*

Doc's family, but she got Doc's birth date wrong – by about 10 years."

Further evidence rests in the fact that census records from 1880 show Doc Holliday residing in Prescott, Arizona, with two other men, one of whom was John Gosper, acting governor of Arizona Territory.

Regardless of the circumstances, Doc did enjoy a long and sometimes combative relationship with Mary Katherine Harony, traveling on many adventures with her. And when it came time to select someone with which to spend his last days as he lay dying in a Glenwood Springs, Colorado, hotel room, it was Mary Katherine Harony to whom he wrote. And it was she who responded and indeed traveled to the high Rockies to care for him until he passed. That's pretty darn close to a marriage.

The Earp Family

As far as Doc Holliday's relationship with the Earp family is concerned, it seems a little hazy too, which is not surprising under the circumstances. After an alliance with the Earps which lasted at least four years, Holliday parted ways with Wyatt in Albuquerque, New Mexico, in 1882. By that time, Morgan Earp – a very close friend of Doc's – had been assassinated in Tombstone, and brother Virgil Earp had also been shot in the back and relegated to a life as a cripple in Los Angeles, California.

"I can't really say if they parted as friends or as friendly enemies," Thomas added. *"I'm not certain, but from everything I can gather, my impression is that they just reached a parting of the ways. Sometimes friendships just reach a point where everything that can be said has been said, and people just go their separate ways. I really think that's probably what happened. Maybe there simply was*

HOTEL GLENWOOD – This accommodation at the corner of 8th Street and Grand Avenue was photographed circa 1887, the year of Holliday's death in a single room on the fifth floor of this structure. Holliday was removed from this room the day of his death and taken to a burial site of unknown specification. (Photo courtesy of Frontier Historical Society)

no reason to continue their partnership after what happened (in the gunfight and its aftermath in Tombstone)."

Thomas suggested the bond between Holliday and the Earps may well have been little more than a friendship of necessity in what then was virtually a lawless environment, making a parting of the ways less than surprising. Documents today indicate that Wyatt and Doc had a falling out over an unflattering comment Doc may have made concerning Wyatt's respect for Jewish traditions. (By that time, Wyatt's bond with his future common-law wife, Josephine Sara Marcus, a Jewess, was quite strong.)

Ms. Thomas also said some insight may be gained into Holliday's life and personality – as well as to his relationship with the Earps – from a letter

Thomas said she received from a very elderly George Earp, dated December 21, 1958. George was a descendant from Nicholas Earp's (patriarch of the Earp brothers) first marriage.

Responding to a letter from the McKey family written after an appearance on *The $64,000 Question*, a television quiz show that year, George Earp wrote Thomas that he had known Holliday for a very brief period in Dodge City.

"When I knew him, he was always a gentlemanly fellow," Earp wrote. *"He was always wanting to die and apparently wanted to be killed. That is why he always wanted to join Wyatt Earp in those gun battles."*

Unfortunately, much – if not all – of the information obtained from George Earp appears to have been falsified in an attempt by the distant Earp to enjoy a portion of the notoriety experienced by his forebears. Today, it is believed that George Earp never even knew Doc Holliday at all.

Bat Masterson

Ms. Thomas has a much more definite opinion about Bat Masterson, who, like the Earps, was allied with Holliday during the heady days of Dodge City, Kansas, where Masterson served as a city marshal.

"For some reason, Bat Masterson didn't like Doc," Thomas asserted. *"He seemed to like the Earps, but he definitely didn't like Doc."*

Ms. Thomas said she also blames much of the Holliday bad press on Masterson, who went on to write about the period known as the "Wild West" in respected publications such as the *New York Times*. After living in the West for many years, Masterson later moved back East to New York where he went to work as a writer for the *Times*. He ultimately died at his desk, a worn-out old man.

"Bat Masterson never wrote anything complimentary about Doc," Thomas added. *"He* (in fact) *made some very disparaging remarks about Doc."*

Though Ms. Thomas did her best to maintain a position as an impartial historian, she said she clearly saw Masterson as a self-serving opportunist eager to secure a place for himself as one of the "heroes" of the period when in fact, some sources describe Masterson's law enforcement skills as lax or worse.

It was a fight from which Ike Clanton had fled in an exceedingly cowardly manner.

"Bat defended himself [in the newspaper] *and he had a big audience. Poor old Doc just died young and had no one to defend him."*

The Haters

Very high on the list of individuals who despised – and would dearly have loved to have maimed or killed – John Henry Holliday, have to be the Clantons and McLaurys of Tombstone fame (or infamy). Ike Clanton in particular made clear that he specifically hated Holliday due to the fact that he (Holliday) constantly mocked and taunted him, and apparently was very adept at taking Clanton's money in poker games.

This hate became particularly intense following the shoot-out behind the O.K. Corral in October of 1881, when Holliday was credited with at least one – and possibly two – of the kills made that day. It was a fight from which Ike Clanton had fled in an exceedingly cowardly manner. Following even more heated exchanges in the later courtroom testimony and open challenges made by Holliday against Ike in the streets of Tombstone, the hate grew incrementally. As a result, few people yearned more to see Holliday dead than Ike Clanton, his brothers, and the McLaury brothers.

Even though he was a small man in stature due to the tuberculosis ravaging his body, John Henry Holliday's amazing hand-speed and deadly accuracy with both a sidearm and knife were put on public display on a number of occasions following his migration to the West. As a result, his reputation shortly began preceding him into whatever town he traveled, and Tombstone was no exception. Though their hate for him was intense, none of the McLaurys or Clantons were willing to publicly attack – or even challenge – Holliday man to man.

Johnny Tyler, also of Tombstone renown, must be included among the intense haters of Holliday. In 1880, shortly after Wyatt Earp's arrival in that town, he forcefully ejected and permanently barred Tyler from the Oriental Saloon. After being thrown into the dusty Tombstone street by Earp, Tyler was taunted by an attending Holliday, and never, for obvious reasons, forgot the incident. Years later, in Leadville, Colorado, he made life miserable for a much weaker and by-then disarmed Doc Holliday.

Another on the haters list has to have been Billy Allen. He was one of the many "wolves" who began circling Holliday in his later years, waiting for an opportunity to make a name for themselves by being the one to snuff out the Georgian's life. He had testified against Holliday and the Earps at the inquest in Tombstone following the noted shootout, and, as fate would have it, also was present in Leadville when Doc – again disarmed and much weaker – took up quarters in that city.

While in Leadville, Allen's strategy had been to loan a then-penniless and desperate Holliday $5.00 when he was too weak to continue earning a living as a regular daily professional card dealer. When Doc was unable to repay the loan, Allen openly abused and publicly insulted him, threatening to give him a beating for failing in repayment. Holliday however – game to the end – was the one who ultimately left Allen bleeding from a gunshot wound on a barroom floor, earning still more hate for the former dentist.

The list goes on and on, but it's pointless to go further. Holliday was small and weak, and as such, he constantly was forced to use his talents with a handgun or other weapons to disabuse bullies of the notion that they could mistreat, insult, and/or harm him. Though this kept his challengers at bay in the early years, it actually did little other than make the list of haters longer and longer.

Movie Portrayals

As far as the movies about Doc Holliday are concerned, Ms. Thomas said she believed actor Val Kilmer – who researched Holliday extensively for his role in the 1993 major motion picture *Tombstone* – may have provided the most accurate portrayal of the man.

"It's obvious that Val thoroughly enjoyed the characterization," Thomas stated. *"Of course, some of what he portrayed was valid and some was not so valid. But it was obvious he had done his homework."*

Thomas said that in general, she regarded almost all the other movies about Holliday to be wildly inaccurate as well as simply poor cinema. She critiqued actor Dennis Quaid's take on Holliday in the 1994 movie *Wyatt Earp* as *"horrible, just horrible. . . an absolute waste of time."*

Another aspect of Holliday's life upon which history buffs disagree wildly is the circumstances of his death. Thomas said a letter, dated June 12, 1973, addressed to her, nailed down with probable finality that information.

The letter quotes A.E. Axtell, city manager of Glenwood Springs, Colorado, where Holliday died on November 8, 1887, after spending two months in and out of consciousness at the Hotel Glenwood. Axtell tells of former Glenwood

Springs Mayor Art Kendricks, who reportedly worked as a busboy at the hotel during the time of Holliday's death.

Last Days

According to Axtell, Kendricks told of carrying bottles of whiskey to Holliday's room and each time being tipped a dime. Kendricks reportedly stated that when Holliday finally died, only the busboy and two others attended the funeral.

This seems to cement Ms. Thomas's argument against Mary Katherine Haroney Cummings (a.k.a. Katie Elder), who claimed she was with Holliday for the last two months of his life. Still, many sources, and at least one credibly-published newspaper account (*Oklahoma Headlight*, February 14, 1899) paint the situation in a different light, stating unequivocally that Kate was indeed present, attending to Holliday and spending what little savings she had to pay the hotel bill, and finally, after his death, gathering Holliday's belongings and shipping them home to his relatives in Georgia.

It is known that Kate was in northwestern Colorado at roughly the same time as Doc's death, since records have been passed down of time she spent in the Crystal Valley region of Colorado near what then was the mining town of Aspen. If she had been that near to Doc during his last days, it is difficult to imagine that she would not at least have paid him a final visit. Further, with her meager funds at that time, it is also unlikely she would have traveled to northwestern Colorado all the way from southern

Kendricks told of carrying bottles of whiskey to Holliday's room and each time being tipped a dime.

Arizona had her destination been of frivolous intent.

And what about the long-standing claim that at the end of his life, Doc regained consciousness just long enough to look at his bare feet and utter the words *"This is funny"* then take one last breath and die?

Ms. Thomas won't even wait for the question about that incident to be finished.

"The man was in a coma!" she exclaimed, when queried. *"Really, I don't think he regained consciousness for those few seconds just to say that."* She clearly considered any such suggestion to be an abject absurdity.

Nevertheless, physicians will explain that invalids on their death-bed will often indeed re-gain consciousness in one final seemingly lucid moment, to perform some action or make some final statement. History is rife with such incidents. It would not have been unusual at all for John Henry Holliday to therefore have made such a statement in his final moments.

And this is exactly the type brief "lucid moment" described in the credible article in the *Oklahoma Headlight* – which was never denied by anyone mentioned in the article – including Glenwood Springs Mayor Art Kendricks. And when one stops to think about it, that brief unique final statement which some – including the *Oklahoma Headlight* article – claim was made by John Henry Holliday is an awfully original-sounding statement for someone to have just manufactured out of thin air.

The Actual Old West Gunfights of John Henry Holliday

The Georgia native was involved in numerous affrays in the Old West over the years, and didn't hesitate to defend himself – usually to great advantage. Nevertheless, many shootings attributed to Doc Holliday either never happened at all, or were simply done by other individuals.

John Henry Holliday was born and raised in the Georgia towns of Griffin and Valdosta. His early life was characterized mainly with the modest, refined and educated life of a Southern gentleman. During these formative years, young John Henry – aside from boyhood pranks – was involved in few if any altercations, and was never a party to any incidents involving gunfights.

Following his diagnosis of tuberculosis and his subsequent relocation to states/territories in the American West, however, the circumstances changed. In stature and muscular development, John Henry at best was a slight and somewhat weak-appearing individual, and his tuberculosis made him even more vulnerable. The Old West was populated by and large with rawhide tough, desperate, and dangerous men, many of whom were constantly seeking an opportunity to establish a reputation, particularly if they could bully another individual.

The weak-appearing John Henry Holliday just naturally became a target of these bullies. It also didn't help matters that the Georgian developed a proclivity for alcohol, gambling, and the saloons in which these vices could be obtained, often becoming inebriated and quarrelsome. It was these circumstances which led to many of his conflicts, since, despite his small stature, John Henry was always "game" for a fight if someone wished to press the issue.

In the instances in which John Henry was challenged, he was anything if defenseless. He carried with him almost constantly several deadly weapons, and didn't hesitate to use them – usually to great success. He was a "dead-shot" with a sidearm, having honed the skill during his youth and into his young adulthood. He also learned to hide and quickly retrieve for use a small knife which he carried with him at all times. Anyone who chose to attempt to assault or bully John Henry Holliday – particularly in his early years out West – had made a serious mistake.

Over the years, as legends grew throughout the Old West, the reputations of many noted gunmen invariably exceeded the actual circumstances of their experiences quite significantly. John

Henry "Doc" Holliday was no exception, being credited with many more shootings and deaths than the ones with which he was actually involved. . . but that did not in any way diminish the fact that he had successfully defended himself on numerous occasions.

According to Karen Holliday Tanner (**Doc Holliday: A Family Portrait**, University of Oklahoma Press, 1998) who has extensively researched the experiences of her famous forebear, Doc can be documented as having been involved in four affrays in which no fatalities occurred:

A gunfight with Charles Austin in Dallas, Texas;

A gunfight with Henry Kahn in Breckenridge, Colorado;

A gunfight with Milt Joyce in Tombstone, Arizona;

A gunfight with Billy Allen in Leadville, Colorado.

Though none of the above shootings involved any fatalities, all resulted in wounded participants – none with the name of Holliday.

Doc was indicted in the Austin case and found *"Not Guilty."*

In the Henry Kahn shooting, Doc was fined, but not charged.

In the shooting incident with Milt Joyce a charge of *"Assault with a Deadly Weapon with Intent to Kill"* was dismissed, and for the misdemeanor charge of *"Assault and Battery"* Doc paid a $20 fine.

In the Billy Allen shooting, Holliday, surprisingly, was charged with

In the instances in which John Henry was challenged, he was anything if defenseless.

"Assault with Intent to Commit Murder," a slightly more serious offense. He was jailed and his bail set at $5,000.00.

In an earlier day, the gunman from Georgia might have easily raised a $5,000.00 bail, but by the time of his days in Leadville, the ex-dentist was a pauper, living virtually hand-to-mouth, and $5,000.00 was an impossibly high amount for him to raise.

Despite his oft-abrasive personality, Holliday seemed to consistently cultivate a coterie of close friends willing to help him in times of need. Two of these – John G. Morgan and Samuel Houston, co-owners of the *Board of Trade Saloon* in Leadville, arrived the morning following his incarceration and posted his bail.

In the trial that followed, a number of eye-witnesses testified to the threats that had been issued at Doc by Allen, and the circumstances of the shooting that had followed. Doc took the stand on his own behalf and explained the details of the incident.

"I saw Allen coming in with his hand in his pocket, and I thought my life was as good to me as his was to him," Holliday explained in his courtroom testimony. *"I fired the shot and he fell on the floor, and (I) fired the second shot; I knew that I would be a child in his hands if he got hold of me; I weigh 122 pounds; I think Allen weighs 170; I have had pneumonia three or four times. I don't think I would have been able to protect myself against him."*

The jury ultimately returned a verdict of *"Not Guilty"* in the case of *People vs John Henry Holliday.*

There were, however, two additional gunfight incidents which did result in the deaths of Holliday's opponents:

At Fort Griffin, Texas, Ed Bailey died at Doc's hand, as did Charlie White in Las Vegas, New Mexico. Despite these deaths, no charges were ever brought against Holliday in these two incidents, so they quite possibly were simply considered obvious cases of self-defense. Both quite likely were more examples of attempts at bullying in which Doc's attackers came to regret – in their final breaths – their actions.

As a result of her research, Ms. Tanner admits that it quite likely was Doc who ended the days of "Old Man" Clanton – the leader of the outlaw Clantons in Tombstone, Arizona Territory in the 1880s, but the details of that incident are sketchy since there were no "extant" witnesses.

It is a documented fact that Doc definitely fired the shot that killed Tom McLaury, and he delivered at least one of the three fatal shots which ended the life of Frank McLaury in the October 26, 1881 shooting near the O.K. Corral in Tombstone, AZ. In this famed Tombstone incident which lasted all of 30 seconds, Ike Clanton, brother to the deceased Billy Clanton who died along with Tom and Frank McLaury, filed murder charges against Virgil, Wyatt and Morgan Earp and John Henry Holliday on October 30, 1881.

> *At Fort Griffin, Texas, Ed Bailey died at Doc's hand, as did Charlie White in Las Vegas, New Mexico.*

In an unusual preliminary hearing for the murder charges, Tombstone Justice of the Peace Wells Spicer heard testimony from a large number of witnesses during the next 30 days, and ultimately concluded there was no basis for a trial. Although he criticized Virgil Earp's use of Wyatt and Holliday as deputies, he concluded that no laws had been violated.

And finally, Doc may or may not have been involved in other killings during what later came to be known as *"the Vendetta Ride,"* when Wyatt and Warren Earp, Doc, Texas Jack Vermillion, Turkey Creek Jack Johnson, Dan Tipton and others sought out the assassins of Morgan Earp and the individuals who attempted to kill Virgil Earp. These vigilante – but necessary – actions ended forever the days of the organized gang of outlaws which had frequented the Tombstone area in the 1870s and early 1880s.

So, if one adds up the obvious cases of record, John Henry Holliday can be credited with ending the lives of at least four men – and quite possibly more, since he was responsible for at least one of the three fatal wounds in Frank McLaury, and he was involved in the Vendetta Ride which definitely resulted in other deaths of unspecified numbers.

Holliday can also be credited with wounding at least five other individuals. Collectively, in the known gunfights in which he was involved, approximately 10 individuals were either killed or wounded.

A Doc Holliday Time-Line In Georgia and the West (1851-1887)

1851: John Henry Holliday was born on August 21, in Griffin, Georgia, to Henry Burroughs Holliday and Alice Jane McKey Holliday.

1864: Major Henry B. Holliday sells all his property and moves his family from Griffin to Valdosta, Georgia, to escape the Union Army troops advancing upon Atlanta.

1866: Alice Jane McKey Holliday, Doc's mother, dies in September, a victim of tuberculosis. John Henry's father remarries a scant three months later, an act which has been described with some import, but which was not uncommon in the least in those days of male spouses with motherless children.

1870: Doc enrolls in the Pennsylvania School of Dental Surgery at Philadelphia.

1872: Doc graduates from dental college.

1873: Doc learns he has tuberculosis. Decides to move to the West, and travels to Dallas, Texas.

1874: Doc is arrested in Dallas for gambling. Moves to Denison, Texas.

1875: In a New Year's Day shooting, Doc is arrested and charged with *"Assault"* and *"Intent to Murder"* Charles Austin in Dallas. He was tried and acquitted. Following his acquittal, he left Dallas, traveled to Fort Griffin, Texas, where he was indicted yet again for gambling.

1876: Doc travels to Denver, Colorado, under the identity of "Tom McKey." He is involved in an altercation and knifes gambler Budd Ryan. Returns to Texas.

1877: Doc is arrested three more times in Dallas for gambling. He later meets Wyatt Earp for the first time at Shaughnessey's Saloon in Fort Griffin. Doc reportedly kills Ed Bailey in Fort Griffin, but no charges were ever lodged, so one must assume the incident was considered a clear-cut case of self-defense.

1878: Doc moves to Dodge City with "Big Nose" Kate Elder (a.k.a. Mary Katherine Harony) where he eventually saves Wyatt Earp's life during an altercation. He shortly travels to Trinidad, Colorado, and Las Vegas, New Mexico, ever the vagabond.

1879: Doc participates in what came to be known as the "Royal Gorge War" during the time of competing railroads being constructed across the United States.

He opens a saloon in Las Vegas. May or may not have been involved in the shooting of Mike Gordon. He is indicted once again for running a gambling operation and carrying a deadly weapon. He decides to leave Las Vegas for Prescott, Arizona with the Earps.

1880: Doc returns to Las Vegas where he shoots Charlie White; the wound, however, is only superficial. No charges were ever brought to bear. He is again arrested for carrying a deadly weapon. Returns to Prescott where he rooms with John J. Gosper, the acting-governor of Arizona Territory. He later moves to Tombstone where he is involved in an altercation with Johnny Tyler and a gunfight and brutal fistfight with Milt Joyce where he is beaten senseless. He, nevertheless manages to shoot Joyce in both the hand and the foot. A charge of *"Assault With A Deadly Weapon With Intent To Kill"* was ultimately dismissed.

1881: Doc provides much-needed assistance to his friend Wyatt as the two defend the arrested "Johnny-Behind-The-Deuce" from a lynch-mob. Doc is accused and arrested for robbery and murder involving a stage coach robbery in Benson, Arizona Territory, but the outlandish charges – leveled by the outlaw Clanton faction – are dismissed upon examination of the circumstances. Doc is involved in what came to be known as the "Gunfight at the O.K. Corral" which ultimately brought both him and the Earps extreme fame. He was arrested

for this shooting and acquitted in the Judge Spicer Hearing and Inquest.

1882: Doc joins Wyatt and Warren Earp, Turkey Creek Jack Johnson, Texas Jack Vermillion, Sherman McMasters, Dan Tipton, and possibly others in what came to be known as the "Vendetta Ride" in Arizona. He was present at the killings of Frank Stillwell, Florentino Cruz, and Curly Bill Brocius, but his actual participation in any of these shootings is unknown. Following these actions, he fled Arizona for New Mexico with the Earp Faction. In Albuquerque, New Mexico, he quarreled with Wyatt Earp during a heated discussion of Earp's latest conquest, Josephine Sarah Marcus. Doc separates from the Earp Faction and travels to Trinidad, New Mexico with Dan Tipton. He eventually leaves there and travels to Denver, Colorado, were he is arrested for extradition back to Arizona. Before the extradition can take place, Doc is rescued by Bat Masterson. He leaves Denver to travel to Gunnison, Salida, Pueblo, and Leadville, Colorado, then back to Denver.

1883-1887: Doc lives much of these four years in Leadville where he is involved in his last gunfight as he shoots Billy Allen in Hyman's Saloon. His arrest for the Billy Allen shooting ultimately goes to trial where he is once again acquitted. Doc travels back and forth to Denver several more times. During his final visit to the Colorado capital, he sees Wyatt Earp for the final time. By this point he is reaching destitution, and is arrested in Denver for vagrancy. Chastened, he returns to Leadville.

1887: Doc had seen enough of Leadville, and decides to move to Glenwood Springs, Colorado, where he finally dies of consumption ("galloping tuberculosis") on November 8, at the age of 36. He reportedly is buried someplace "near Linwood Cemetery" in Glenwood Springs. The exact site of his final remains is a total mystery today.

Though some commercial structures on this central avenue have been replaced over the years, the former San Miguel Valley Bank building (2nd from left) lives on in downtown Telluride, Colorado. (Photo by Olin Jackson)

The San Miguel Valley Bank building (2nd from right) in Telluride CO is pictured at about the same time as it was robbed by famed outlaw Robert LeRoy Parker (a.k.a. Butch Cassidy) on June 24, 1889. His escape route was a well-traveled ancient trail down through the San Juan Mountains, and is the same as would have been used by many adventurers of that day, including John Henry Holliday and the Earp brothers circa 1882-1883.

The Final Disposition
Of His Old West Friends

*Though his life was cut short by tuberculosis, John Henry Holliday's closest friends –
the Earp family – lived considerably longer, with many of them ultimately expiring in
California where they occupy numerous gravesites today.*

Though the lives they lived were dangerous beyond description, the Earp brothers – several of whom were considered the best friends of John Henry Holliday – lived far beyond the death of the dentist from Georgia. But just as did Holliday, the Earps traveled far and wide in the old West in search of livelihood and adventure. Wyatt eventually even traveled as far as Gnome, Alaska, where he lived for several years. Prior to that time and following their departure from Arizona Territory in 1882, James, Virgil, Wyatt and Warren and their common-law wives all resided for a number of years in California in the Colton/San Bernardino vicinity.

Colton Crossing outside Colton, California, was the site of one of the more notable "frog wars" in American railroad history. A frog war occured when one private (and early) railroad company found itself in need of constructing its rail line across the tracks of another major rail line, particularly as the trans-continental rail lines were being constructed across the western continental United States. It was a situation which inevitably resulted in hostilities between the two competing railroads.

In the summer of 1882 (just a few months following the famed gunfight behind the O.K. Corral in Tombstone, Arizona Territory), tensions reached their boiling point when construction of the tracks for the *California Southern Railroad* reached Colton, California. In an attempt to forcibly prevent the competing California Southern crews from completion of their line which intersected the tracks of the *Southern Pacific (SP)*, a SP locomotive and gondola were parked on the tracks at the location of the planned crossing. In addition, the *SP* hired armed men, including the by-then well-known Virgil Earp of Tombstone fame, to guard the tracks. Competition for control of the major east-west routes of the rails was big and valuable business.

Before the growing potential for violence at the Colton crossing could get out of hand, Governor Robert Waterman ordered San Bernardino County Sheriff J.B. Burkhart to enforce a state court order for completion of Cal Southern's route. Waterman informed Earp of the court order, causing the former lawman to acquiesce and instruct the *SP* engineer to remove its locomotive where it was blocking the intersection. The crossing then was built, ending the Southern Pacific's monopoly in Southern California.

<u>COLTON, CALIFORNIA</u> **(circa 1890)** – Pictured is dusty and quiet 8th Street in downtown Colton. It was here that the Earp family lived and worked in the taverns and other enterprises, after moving from Missouri. Following the bad days in Tombstone, Arizona, in the early 1880s, James and Virgil Earp relocated to this town, later to be followed by brothers Wyatt and Warren. The nearby Santa Fe Railroad with its major rail yard and depot was regularly patronized by the Earps in many of their travels.

The Earps in California

Nicholas Earp, patriarch of the by-then famed Earp family had initially arrived in San Bernardino County, California, from their former home in Lamar, Missouri, on December 17, 1864. They remained in the vicinity, living on a small farm for approximately four years until 1868 when they inexplicably returned to Lamar.

Most of the early migrations of the Earp family (and there were several) back and forth between California and Missouri were made via covered wagon, since there was no railroad or other mode of transportation from the eastern United States (or elsewhere) to California until 1869. These trips were made under extremely dangerous circumstances, since the western interior of the nation at that time was still an extremely wild and remote country largely controlled by hostile native Indians, and populated by millions of buffalo and other wildlife.

In 1877, Nicholas and family returned to San Bernardino, this time with youngest son *Warren* – who was twenty-three years of age at the time – in tow. Warren did not initially share the adventures of his older brothers in Kansas and Arizona, choosing instead to remain in the shadow of his parents in California during his early years.

As a result of his very aggressive personality, the family often referred to young Warren fondly as "the tiger." Unfortunately, this undesirable personality trait would gradually evolve into a bullying and very abusive behavior which he imposed upon almost everyone with whom he came into contact, particularly if he (Warren) was under the influence of alcohol – which was often. It ultimately

VIRGIL EARP HOME – The domicile once occupied by Virgil and Allie Earp at 528 West "H" Street in Colton, California, is pictured. It was here that Virgil and Allie resided for a number of years while he served as marshal of Colton and engaged in other business endeavors. Though crippled in his left arm by an assassination attempt in Tombstone, Arizona Territory in 1881, he nevertheless was still a dependable and effective law enforcement officer for a number of years.

WARREN EARP (circa 1883) – Nellie "Bessie" Bartlett Ketcham Earp was married to oldest brother James Earp. She was a modestly attractive female who had nevertheless lived a hard life, reflected in her no-nonsense uncompromising gaze. She is pictured here with the youngest Earp brother, Warren. Prior to (and possibly even after) meeting James, Bessie was a prostitute which was not uncommon in those days in the West. She died prematurely at the age of 47 in January of 1887 in Colton, and was buried in San Bernardino's *Pioneer Memorial Cemetery*. Warren was so roundly disliked by virtually all his acquaintances that when he was murdered in 1900 in Willcox, Arizona, he was hastily buried in an unmarked grave and forgotten. The specific site of his grave today is unknown.

was largely responsible for ending his life prematurely.

According to the **San Bernardino Index** newspaper, *"Warren Earp of Colton, while intoxicated, entered the French restaurant on D Street and called for a supper. While his order was being prepared and before it was served, he became very noisy and tried to break the bottles in the caster. The night steward spoke* to him politely and told him to keep quiet or else go out. At this Earp turned to and began to abuse the steward, raising up and striking him in the face at the same time. Earp struck the steward on the arm with a pickle jar, shattering the bottle and lacerating the waiter's arm and hand in a fearful manner. Officer Thomas was called in and placed Earp under arrest."

Over the course of the next nine years – well into the 1880s – Warren reportedly was involved in at least three major bar fights at sites in San Bernardino County which were recorded as news items. In one incident, he shot off the right thumb of his antagonist – a man named Jones. In another, he faced off against two Mexicans, waging war against them with a wooden club with which he reportedly imposed serious injury upon one of the men.

All three participants in this wooden club melee were arrested, but as was

SANTA FE RAILROAD – The Depot for this rail line in San Bernardino was photographed here in 1915. It was one of the busiest rail yards in the Southwest at the time, and was occasionally used by the Earp family in their travels.

often the case, father Nicholas was there to bail Warren out of jail that same night. That fatherly over-protection, it appears, was responsible to a great degree for Warren's descent into unpredictable and socially-unacceptable behavior. He seldom, if ever, was required to pay a price for his transgressions.

The other Earp siblings – *James, Virgil, Wyatt* and *Morgan* – had departed from the family nest well prior to Nicholas's arrival in San Bernardino to pursue various other occupational opportunities – usually in law enforcement, saloon operation, or mining – in neighboring states. Though some of them would later temporarily take up residence in and around San Bernardino, none – save James and Morgan – would ultimately die and be buried in that vicinity.

In 1880, *Nicholas* and wife, *Virginia*, and *Warren* moved yet again, this time to nearby Colton where the elder Earp purchased a farm outside of town

which became the center of Earp operations for a number of years. He also purchased a saloon in Colton which he named the "Gem." Warren, as befitted his personality, became a bartender in this saloon for a period of time.

Since he had a legal background – having served earlier in Missouri as a judge – Nicholas was able to apply this knowledge to several occupations associated with the legal profession in the Colton and San Bernardino areas, including service as justice of the peace in Colton. As such, he interacted on a regular basis with the Colton populace for many years.

All of Nicholas's sons and their various wives lived on and off in Colton from the 1870s through the 1930s, until their deaths or migrations to other locales eliminated their Colton residence.

On October 26, 1881, Virgil, Wyatt, and Morgan were involved in the aforementioned famous and epic gunfight behind the O.K. Corral in Tombstone,

SAN GABRIEL MOUNTAINS – The "California Limited" on the Santa Fe is a good example of the rail transportation available in the days of Doc Holliday and the Earp family. This photo was made at Cajon Summit, the highest point on the rail line between the San Bernardino Mountains to the east and the San Gabriel Mountains to the west in Southern California.

Arizona Territory, which resulted in three deaths. Their lives were never the same from that point forward.

Final Days of the Earps

On March 18, 1882, in an attempt to eliminate what remained of the ever-vigilant and rigorous Earp law-enforcement cabal remaining in Tombstone, several members of the "Cow Boy" outlaw group assassinated *Morgan Earp* as he played billiards in Hatch's Saloon and narrowly missed placing a round in *Wyatt* as well as he sat watching the game.

James and his wife, "*Bessie*," accompanied Morgan's body back to Colton where he was buried in that town's *Slover Mountain Cemetery*. When, five years later, quarrying operations encroached upon Morgan's remains in *Slover*, he was relocated to nearby *Hermosa Garden Cemetery*.

Morgan's beautiful wife, *Louisa "Lou" Houston Earp* reportedly had actually left Morgan earlier in Tombstone and traveled to Colton to live after discovering that he had another consort in

the Tombstone area. Louisa therefore never again saw Morgan alive after leaving Tombstone. She, also, unfortunately died prematurely in 1894 in Long Beach, California, at age 39. She was buried in *Evergreen Cemetery* in Los Angeles.

No doubt sensing his brothers' need for support in Tombstone in 1881 following the rising tensions there, *Warren* had relocated from Colton to Arizona during this period for a short time, but just as in Colton, his trouble-prone ways continued to follow him as he was involved in dangerous incident after incident. He, nevertheless, teamed up in Tombstone with brother Wyatt and his law enforcement associates to support them as the outlaw element became more determined than ever in their efforts to eliminate the Earp faction.

Later, in 1882, after ridding the southern Arizona Territory of many of the outlaws residing there, Wyatt and Warren, accompanied by *John Henry Holliday*, "*Texas Jack*" *Vermillion*, "*Turkey Creek*" *Jack Johnson*, *Dan Tipton*, and one or two others departed that

SAN BERNARDINO (1884) – The sleepy rustic status of old San Bernardino, California, was captured in this photo. The railroad is visible mid-frame. Colton is a suburb of San Bernardino, and various members of the Earp family resided in both locales. (Photo courtesy of San Bernardino Public Library)

vicinity, traveling to New Mexico, Colorado, Idaho, California, and other locales in a constant search for adventure and sources of income.

Warren eventually returned to the Colton/San Bernardino environs to live a short while with brothers Virgil, James, and other members of his family, but he eventually tired of life in Colton (or else had worn-out his welcome there) and returned, surprisingly, to Arizona, where he was hired by a cattle business near Willcox. In one of the last photos taken of him, he is pictured (either in Tombstone or Colton) with James's wife, Bessie.

In 1900, *Warren*'s penchant for trouble finally caught up with him in a fatal manner, resulting in his shooting

NEWTON EARP – Newton was the son of Nicholas Earp and his first wife, Abigail Storm. As such, he was a half-brother to James, Virgil, Wyatt, Morgan and Warren and sisters Martha, Adelia, Virginia and Mariah. Residing in numerous locales from Missouri to Nevada, Newton spent much of his later life in north California, but lived for a short time in San Bernardino. Despite his half-brother status to his famed male siblings, Newton was very close with his brothers his entire life.

death in a saloon in Willcox following a drunken argument. He and range boss **Johnny Boyette** had engaged in numerous violent confrontations in recent months, and had both become extremely hostile to the opposite party. Finally, following threats of violence by Earp, Boyette reportedly drew his revolver without provocation, and shot Warren in cold blood, killing him instantly.

Just as he had been in Colton, San Bernardino, and Tombstone, the youngest Earp was so roundly disliked in Willcox that no law enforcement authorities ever even attempted to arrest Boyette, nor were any charges filed against him nor even any investigation made of the shooting.

Warren Earp was buried in an unmarked grave in *Willcox Pioneer Cemetery* (no doubt to eliminate the possibility of a coroner's inquest to determine Boyette's guilt or innocence). It was recorded by a number of sources that Warren was clearly unarmed at the time of the shooting. The exact site of his grave was never marked, though the cemetery in which his remains reside at least is known. A similar fate had earlier befallen

Boyette reportedly drew his revolver without provocation, and shot Warren in cold blood, killing him instantly.

It was recorded by a number of sources that Warren was clearly unarmed at the time of the shooting.

John Henry Holliday in Glenwood Springs, Colorado.

Following the Tombstone misfortunes and his later crippling wounds from an attempt on his life in that town on December 28 of 1881, **U.S. Deputy Marshal Virgil Earp** had decided a change of venue was in order and he moved from Tombstone to Colton where he resided with wife, **Alvira "Allie" Packingham Sullivan**, at 528 West "H" Street. This home, now a historic site, still stands in Colton as of this writing (2023).

Despite his devastated left arm which hung useless by his side for the remainder of his life, Virgil nevertheless was still effective as a law enforcement officer. He opened a detective agency in Colton, and, in 1886, was elected the town constable. When Colton was incorporated as a city, Virgil was elected as the first City Marshal on July 11, 1887. He was paid $75 a month and was re-elected to another term in 1888.

In later 1888, Virgil resigned as city marshal and he and Allie strangely left Colton for nearby San Bernardino. Five years later, in 1893, he and Allie moved yet again to the short-lived mining town of Vanderbilt, California, where he owned and operated *Earp's Hall*, a saloon, gambling hall, and meeting place used for public gatherings and even the town's weekly church services. His successes in the political arena in Vanderbilt, however, did not rise to the level of his previous electoral endeavors, since he lost the election for town constable in 1894.

In 1895, the San Bernardino City and County Directories carried the following listings: *San Bernardino Section: Earp, Warren – Capitalist. Earp, Virgil W. – Saloon Keeper. Colton Section: Earp, Nicholas P. – Book Agent.*

In 1901, **Virgil** and **Wyatt** attempted to open a gambling hall in Colton, but the town fathers voted down the enterprise, much to the two brothers' disappointment. The two continued nevertheless with other business endeavors in the Colton/San Bernardino area for several years, as well as in a number of other states and locales.

In 1905, **Virgil's** hard life finally caught up with him when, at age 62, he came down with and died from pneumonia. As an inveterate cigar-smoker, his tobacco affinity had not aided his attempt at recovery from the pneumococcal bacteria with which his lungs were infected. Since his first wife and child lived in Portland, Oregon, Virgil's body was shipped there by rail for burial in that city's *Riverview Cemetery*.

In February of 1907 in Colton, **Nicholas Earp**, patriarch of the Earp family who had lived to the ripe old age of 94, finally succumbed to the rigors of life. As a veteran of the Black Hawk and Mexican American wars, Nicholas was entitled to free burial at a nearby military cemetery.

Nicholas's wife – **Virginia Anne Cooksey Earp** – died in San Bernardino and is buried in the *Pioneer Memorial Cemetery* in that town.

In January of 1926, **James Earp**, the oldest full brother who had survived the U.S. Civil War as well, as well as the troubles in Tombstone, Arizona, where he had been a barkeeper, died quietly in San Bernardino at age 84. He was buried in that city's *Mountain View Cemetery*.

James's beautiful wife, **Nellie "Bessie" Bartlett Ketcham Earp** had died prematurely in January of 1887, in Colton, at the relatively young age of 47. She was buried in San Bernardino's *Pioneer Memorial Cemetery* as well, not far from her mother-in-law, Virginia Anne Cooksey Earp.

On December 18, 1928, at the advanced age of 91, **Newton Earp** passed away in Sacramento, California. Born in 1837 in Ohio County, Kentucky, Newton was the son of Nicholas Earp and his first wife, **Abigail Storm**. As such, he was a half-brother to James, Virgil, Wyatt, Morgan and Warren and sisters **Martha**, **Adelia**, **Virginia** and **Mariah**. Despite his half-brother status to his famed male siblings, Newton was very close with his brothers his entire life.

Following service in the Union Army during the U.S. Civil War, Newton

In 1905, Virgil's hard life finally caught up with him when, at age 62, he came down with and died from pneumonia.

had returned home and married *Jane "Jennie" Adam* in Marion County, Missouri, in 1865. The newlyweds then joined patriarch Nicholas and siblings in Southern California's San Bernardino. There, Newton worked as a saloon manager.

Prostate cancer took the famed lawman just short of his 81st birthday

The elder brother later returned with his wife and children to the Midwest in 1868, first settling in Lamar, Missouri, where he became a farmer. Finding himself unsuited for that profession, Newton relocated with his wife and family to Kansas. Just as with all the other members of his later-renowned family, Newton was a wanderer.

Newton and Jennie ultimately became the parents of five children: *Effie May*, *Wyatt Clyde*, *Mary Elizabeth*, *Alice Abigail*, and *Virgil Edwin*. The couple obviously named their first-born son (born August 25, 1872) after his not-yet-famous uncle, Wyatt, and their second son (born April 19, 1880) after his equally not-yet-famous uncle, Virgil.

Following another relocation to California, Newton became a carpenter, building homes in northern California and northwestern Nevada. Newton's wife, Jennie, died on March 29, 1898, in Paradise Hill, Nevada (also known as "Paradise Valley").

Only his half-brother Wyatt and half-sister Adelia outlived Newton, with Wyatt dying approximately one month later on January 13, 1929.

Wyatt's famous last utterances as he passed away were "Suppose. Suppose."

Newton is buried in Sacramento's *East Lawn Memorial Park* cemetery.

In 1929, despite all the many dangerous engagements and gunfights which he had survived in his life, *Wyatt Berry Stapp Earp* finally was himself felled, but not by an outlaw's or assassin's bullet. Prostate cancer took the famed lawman just short of his 81st birthday in Los Angeles, California. During his life he had been a buffalo hunter, lawman, gambling table manager, saloon keeper, miner, boxing referee, gambler, and brothel keeper, to name a few of his occupations.

Wyatt's famous last utterances as he passed away were *"Suppose. Suppose."* If they were understood by those in his presence at the time, the cryptic final words were never explained. Wyatt was cremated and his ashes were interred in Colma, a suburb of San Francisco, California, in a Jewish cemetery where wife, *Josephine*, was later buried alongside him.

Virgil Earp's common-law wife (who was actually his second spouse) – *Alvira* – died in November of 1947. She had weathered all the tough years with the Earps, including the shoot-outs in Tombstone and elsewhere, outliving her husband by 42 years. She was one of the last original Earps in Colton, and was buried with a number of the other Earp family members in Colton's *Mountain View Cemetery*.

About The Author

R. Olin Jackson founded *Legacy Communications, Inc.*, in 1985, where he became the award-winning executive editor and publisher of his flagship creations – *North Georgia Journal* and *Georgia Backroads* magazines. He ultimately built these endeavors into the premier travel and history publications of Georgia.

During his tenure at *Legacy Communications*, Olin was the recipient of a number of awards from the *Magazine Association of Georgia (MAG)* for excellence in publishing. He parlayed this business endeavor into a long and fruitful career before selling it in 2005. *Georgia Backroads* is now in its 38th year (as of 2024) of publication, and is one of the longest-running magazines in the state.

In the interim of his work at Legacy Communications, Olin also wrote/co-wrote a selection of books, including *Moonshine, Murder and Mayhem in Georgia* (2003); *Tales of the Rails in Georgia* (2004); and *Georgia Backroads Traveler* (2005) among others.

In 2021, Olin founded *Whippoorwill Publications, LLC*. His creations there include *Mystery & History in Georgia, Volume I* (2022) (honored with a *Five-Star Award* by *Readers' Favorite* book awards); *Mystery & History in Georgia, Volume II* (2023); *Some Genealogy Keys to Some Georgia Family*

Trees (2023); and *Memories of Army Life and MPs of the 529th* (2023). Other works in progress include a captivating novel of historic fiction entitled *Whippoorwill Hill*; and a selection of original poetry entitled *After All That We've Been Through*.

Olin is married to the former Judy Grizzle of Dahlonega, Georgia. The couple make their home in Roswell, Georgia. Olin also has a son – Burke – by a former marriage.

All works by *Whippoorwill Publications* are available online at *Amazon.com*, *IngramSpark.com*, *BarnesandNoble.com*, and other fine booksellers.

Supplemental
Bibliographical References

1/ Carlisle, Gene, *Why Doc Holliday Left Georgia* (2004), Carl Isle Publishing, Inc.,

2/ Churchill, E. Richard, *Doc Holliday, Bat Masterson, & Wyatt Earp, Their Colorado Careers* (2001), Western Reflections Publishing Company

3/ Clavin, Tom, *Tombstone: The Earp Brothers, Doc Holliday, and the Vendetta Ride From Hell* (2020), St. Martin's Press, New York

4/ Clavin, Tom, *Dodge City: Wyatt Earp, Bat Masterson and the Wickedest Town in the American West* (2017), St. Martin's Press, New York

5/ DeMattos, Jack, *Mysterious Gunfighter: The Story of Dave Mather* (1992), Creative Publishing Co., College Station, Texas

6/ Earp, Josephine Sarah Marcus, *I Married Wyatt Earp* (1976), University of Arizona Press, Tucson, AZ

7/ Furnas, J.C., *The Americans: A Social History of the United States, 1587-1914* (1969), G.P. Putnam's Sons, New York

8/ Garrett, Franklin and Rice, Bradley, *Atlanta History, A Journal of the South* (1980), Atlanta Historic Society

9/ Hicks, John D., *The Federal Union (Second Edition), A History of the United States to 1865* (1952), Houghton Mifflin Company / Riverside Press, Cambridge

10/ Jackson, III, Ralph Olin, *A North Georgia Journal of History, Vol. 1* (1989), Legacy Communications, Inc.

11/ Jackson, III, Ralph Olin, *A North Georgia Journal of History, Vol. 2* (1991), Legacy Communications, Inc.

12/ Jackson, III, Ralph Olin, *A North Georgia Journal of History, Vol. 3* (1995), Legacy Communications, Inc.

13/ Jackson, III, Ralph Olin, *A North Georgia Journal of History, Vol. 4* (1999), Legacy Communications, Inc.

14/ Jackson, III, Ralph Olin, *Georgia's Doc Holliday* (2006), Whippoorwill Publications, LLC, Roswell, GA

15/ Jackson, III, Ralph Olin, *Moonshine, Murder & Mayhem in Georgia* (2003), Legacy Communications, Inc.

16/ Jackson, III, Ralph Olin, *Tales of the Rails in Georgia* (2004), Legacy Communications, Inc.

17/ Lubet, Steven, *Murder In Tombstone: The Forgotten Trial of Wyatt Earp* (2004), Yale University Press, New Haven and London

18/ Meadows, Anne, *Digging Up Butch and Sundance* (1994), St. Martin's Press, New York

19/ Metz, Leon Claire, *The Shooters* (1976), Mangan Books

20/ Meyers, John Meyers, *Tombstone's Early Years* (1950), University of Nebraska Press, Lincoln and London

21/ Nelson, Jim, *Glenwood Springs: A Quick History* (1998), Blue Chicken Publishing, Glenwood Springs, CO

22/ Nelson, Jim, *Glenwood Springs: The History of a Rocky Mountain Resort* (1999), Western Reflections, Inc., Ouray, Colorado

23/ Rosa, Joseph G., *Wild Bill Hickok, Gunfighter* (2001), Creative Publishing Company, College Station, TX

24/ Swanson, Doug J., *Cult of Glory: The*

Bold and Brutal History of The Texas Rangers (2020), Viking Press.

25/ Tanner, Karen Holliday, ***Doc Holliday: A Family Portrait*** (1998), University of Oklahoma Press, Norman, OK

26/ Tefertiller, Casey, ***Wyatt Earp: The Life Behind The Legend*** (1990), John Wiley & Sons, New York

27/ Turner, Alford E., ***The Earps Talk*** (1980), Creative Publishing Company, College Station, Texas

28/ Williams, Harry T.; Current, Richard N.; and Freidel, Frank; ***A History of the United States to 1876*** (1959), Alfred A. Knopf, New York

Full Name Index

Topic Index